TRAINING

Haupt-/Mittelschule

Englisch 9. Klasse

Monika Wanders
Philip Prowse

Autoren:

Monika Wanders verfügt über eine langjährige Berufserfahrung als Lehrerin und als Ausbilderin von Lehramtsanwärtern und Studenten der Ludwig-Maximilians-Universität München (Schwerpunkt Englischunterricht).

Philip Prowse ist international bekannt als Autor von Englisch-Lernmaterialien und Lehrwerken.

© 2022 STARK Verlag GmbH, St.-Martin-Straße 82, 81541 München
www.stark-verlag.de
1. Auflage 2009

Inhalt

Fortsetzung siehe nächste Seite

Autoren: Monika Wanders und Philip Prowse
Illustrator: Rainer Thiele

Vorwort

Liebe Schülerin, lieber Schüler,

wir gratulieren dir zu deiner Entscheidung, dich **aktiv** um das Lernen der englischen Sprache zu bemühen. Mit diesem Buch kannst du das Grundwissen der 9. Klasse wiederholen, deinen Kenntnisstand überprüfen und dich auf Tests oder Prüfungen vorbereiten. Es besteht aus vier Teilen:

▶ Das Kapitel **Topics and tasks** bildet den Hauptteil des Buches: Hier findest du **Texte** und **Aufgaben**, mit denen du die **sprachlichen Kompetenzen** Leseverstehen, Wortschatz, Grammatik, und Schreiben trainieren kannst.

▶ Das Kapitel **Checkpoint** enthält Aufgaben zu allen behandelten Grammatikthemen. Du kannst es als **Test** verwenden, um deinen Kenntnisstand zu prüfen.

▶ Unter **Vocabulary** findest du eine **Vokabelliste** mit schwierigen Wörtern, die in diesem Buch verwendet werden, und eine Liste der wichtigsten **unregelmäßigen Verben**.

▶ Das Kapitel **Key** enthält zu allen Aufgaben **ausführliche Lösungen**, damit du deine eigene Leistung kontrollieren kannst.

Auch wenn's mitunter schwer fällt – gib nicht auf! Denn Englisch ist eine **Weltsprache**, die dir in deinem Leben noch oft nützlich sein wird – egal ob im Urlaub oder in deinem zukünftigen Beruf.

Wir wünschen dir viel Erfolg und Freude bei der Arbeit mit diesem Buch!

All the best from the authors …

Monika Wanders

Philip Prowse

Topics and tasks

Dieses Kapitel enthält neun gleich aufgebaute **Themen** *(topics)* mit vielen abwechslungsreichen **Aufgabenstellungen** *(tasks)*, die nach Kompetenzbereichen geordnet sind:

▶ **Reading:** Mit den **Working on the text**-Aufgaben kannst du prüfen, ob du den **Lesetext** verstanden hast.

▶ **Language:** Dieser Teil enthält vielfältige **Wortschatzübungen**.

▶ **Grammar:** Hier werden **grammatische Themen** anschaulich erklärt und anschließend anhand vielfältiger **Aufgaben** eingeübt.

▶ **Text Production:** In diesem Abschnitt **verfasst du selbst längere Texte**, z. B. Briefe. **Sprachliche Mittel** helfen dir, in bestimmten Situationen schriftlich und mündlich die passenden Formulierungen zu finden.

Topic 1: Carnivals around the world

1 Everyone has heard of the carnival in Rio in Brazil, but not everyone knows that Europe's largest carnival takes place not in Spain, Greece, or Germany but in London. Carnival came to Notting Hill from the Caribbean, particularly Trinidad, over thirty-five years ago. The Notting Hill Carnival welcomes tourists
5 and has as its motto 'Every spectator is a participant – Carnival is for all who dare to participate.' The Notting Hill Carnival is truly multi-cultural with groups from all over the world, including Afghanistan, Bangladesh, Russia and Brazil as well as all parts of the Caribbean, South America and Africa.

See the reality behind the movie! The film *Notting Hill* shows us a smart
10 quiet part of London. But the Carnival shows you another Notting Hill, the most fantastic weekend in London's year.

For two days at the end of August every year a million people come to Notting Hill. More than fifty 'Mas' bands and as many 'Sound Systems' play. The bands are followed through the streets by thousands of people. Dancing makes
15 you hungry and exotic food from all over the world is an important feature of this carnival.

But the world's biggest carnival is in Rio de Janeiro. People celebrate carnival in February or March all over Brazil, and festivals are different in each region. But the week-long Carnival in Rio is special. It's the world's best-known carni-
20 val and millions of people go to it.

The sixteen main *escolas de samba* (the samba schools) work all year, preparing for the two nights of parades in the *sambodromo* (the giant samba stadium). Each school has thousands of dancers in its parade and 600 to 800 drummers. It's the loudest music you're ever likely to hear in your life. The dancers all wear
25 the most amazing costumes and each samba school takes about an hour and a half to go by the judges. The Carnival parades take ten to twelve hours each and the judges choose the best samba school. When it's Carnival, Rio is not only the most exciting city in the world, but it is also one of the most expensive, with hotel and taxi prices up by 400 %!

Vocabulary

particularly (line 3): *besonders*
spectator (line 5): *Zuschauer/in*
participant (line 5): *Teilnehmer/in*
to dare (line 6): *wagen, sich trauen*
to participate (line 6): *teilnehmen, mitmachen*
smart (line 9): *hier: gepflegt, elegant*
feature (line 16): *Merkmal, (Haupt-)Attraktion*
amazing (line 25): *erstaunlich, verblüffend*
judge (line 27): *(Preis-)Richter*in*

Working on the text

1 Tick (✓) the right answer.

  a The Notting Hill Carnival started …

    ☐ over fifty years ago.

    ☐ less than ten years ago.

    ☐ over thirty-five years ago.

    ☐ less than twenty years ago.

  b The groups at the Notting Hill Carnival come …

    ☐ just from England.

    ☐ from all over the world.

    ☐ just from the Caribbean.

    ☐ from all over Europe.

c How many 'Sound Systems' are there at the Notting Hill Carnival?

☐ over fifty

☐ a million

☐ just three

☐ about a hundred

d The largest carnival on Earth takes place in ...

☐ London.

☐ Germany.

☐ Trinidad.

☐ Brazil.

e At the Rio Carnival the judges see each samba school for about ...

☐ two nights.

☐ 90 minutes.

☐ ten hours.

☐ twelve hours

f At Carnival time in Rio everything ...

☐ costs the same as usual.

☐ is cheaper than usual.

☐ is a little more expensive than usual.

☐ is much more expensive than usual.

2 True, false or not in the text?

		true	false	not in the text
a	Notting Hill is in Trinidad.	☐	☐	☐
b	The film *Notting Hill* is about the carnival.	☐	☐	☐
c	Notting Hill Carnival is in the summer.	☐	☐	☐
d	The weather in Rio is very hot at carnival.	☐	☐	☐
e	The samba schools spend two days preparing for the Rio Carnival.	☐	☐	☐
f	The Rio Carnival is very noisy.	☐	☐	☐

Language

3 Form four sentences that fit the text. Use each part of the sentence only once.

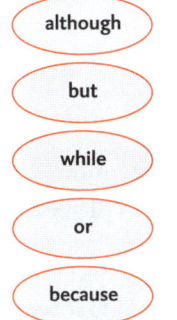

The Notting Hill Carnival is multi-cultural	*although*	listen to the music from three live stages.
People visit Carnival in Rio de Janeiro	*but*	Europe's largest carnival isn't well known.
Carnival in Rio is famous all over the world	*while*	it's very expensive.
Tourists can follow one of the parades	*or*	groups from all over the world take part.
	because	

4 Cross out the word that doesn't fit and find the collective noun.

a hammer – saw – drill – ~~wood~~   → *tools*

b Italy – Great Britain – Russian – Brazil → _____

c artist – teach – dancer – singer   → _____

d Italian – Germany – French – Spanish   → _____

e uncle – housewife – cousin – sister   → _____

5 Underline the word which is closest in meaning to the first two words in each line.

a brilliant – excellent   <u>great</u> – funny – dangerous

b love – like   listen – hate – enjoy

c keen – enthusiastic   careful – eager – strong

d whole – total   hole – money – everything

e region – area   neighbour – road – district

Grammar

Steigerung von Adjektiven

Mit den Steigerungsformen des Adjektivs kannst du verschiedene **Abstufungen von Eigenschaften** ausdrücken.

Beispiel:	Peter is <u>strong</u>.	(Grundform)	Peter ist stark.
	James is <u>stronger</u>.	(1. Steigerungsform)	James ist stärker.
	Anne is the <u>strongest</u>.	(2. Steigerungsform)	Anne ist die Stärkste.

Wie bildest du die Steigerungsformen?

- Die meisten **einsilbigen und zweisilbigen Adjektive** bilden ihre Steigerungsformen durch Anhängen der **Endungen -er** bzw. **-est** an die Grundform.
  Beispiel: great – great<u>er</u> – the great<u>est</u>

  Beachte folgende **Ausnahmen bei der Schreibung:**
  - Bei Adjektiven, die auf -y enden, wird das -y zu -i.
    Beispiel: funny – funn<u>ier</u> – the funn<u>iest</u>
  - Bei Adjektiven mit einem kurzen betonten Vokal verdoppelt sich der Endkonsonant.
    Beispiel: hot – hot<u>ter</u> – the hot<u>test</u>
  - Bei Adjektiven, die auf -e enden, fügst du nur ein -r bzw. -st an.
    Beispiel: large – larg<u>er</u> – the larg<u>est</u>

- Bei **mehrsilbigen Adjektiven** fügst du more bzw. most ein.
  Beispiel: fantastic – <u>more</u> fantastic – the <u>most</u> fantastic

- Einige Adjektive haben **unregelmäßige Steigerungsformen**. Diese Adjektive und ihre Formen musst du auswendig lernen.
  Beispiel: good – <u>better</u> – the <u>best</u>

6 Fill in the blanks with the right form of the adjectives.

amazing	_more amazing_	(the) most amazing
_____	_____	(the) prettiest
expensive	_____	_____
_____	more fantastic	_____
quiet	_____	_____
noisy	_____	_____
_____	more important	_____
elegant	_____	_____
spectacular	_____	_____
_____	_____	(the) largest

> **Vergleich von Adjektiven**
> Um auszudrücken, dass Dinge **gleich, ungleich** oder **unterschiedlich** sind, verwendest du Vergleiche.
> *Beispiel:* London is <u>bigger than</u> Birmingham.
> **Wie bildest du Vergleiche (*comparisons*)?**
> - Wenn Dinge **gleich** sind, verwendest du *as* + Grundform des Adjektivs + *as*.
>   *Beispiel:* John is <u>as tall as</u> Peter.
> - Wenn Dinge **ungleich** sind, verwendest du *not* + *as* + Grundform des Adjektivs + *as*.
>   *Beispiel:* Peter is <u>not as tall as</u> Sarah.
> - Wenn zwei Dinge **unterschiedlich** sind, verwendest du die 1. Steigerungsform des Adjektivs + *than*.
>   *Beispiel:* Sarah is <u>taller than</u> John.

7 Form comparisons.

a A plane is ____*faster*____ than a car.

b A horror film is _____ (exciting) than a documentary film.

c Walking is _____ (slow) than in-line skating.

d Commercials are _____ (funny) than news.

e A trip to New York is

_____

(expensive) than a flight to London.

8 After their visit to the Notting Hill Carnival Anne and Peter are comparing it with other events. Find the right forms of the adjectives.

a The live event was much ____*nicer than*____ (nice) carnival on TV.

b London is _____ (big) Rio de Janeiro.

c The music in the streets is _____ (loud) in the *sambodromo*.

d Carnival in Rio is the world's _____ (spectacular) carnival.

e Notting Hill Carnival is Europe's _____ (good) street party.

f The number of spectators in Rio is _____ (high) in London.

g At Carnival in Rio the hotels and taxis are _____ (expensive) than usual.

h At carnival, Rio is _____ (exciting) city of the world.

i The dancers in the samba parades wear _____ (amazing) costumes _____ you could ever see anywhere else.

Text Production

> **Sprachliche Mittel: Wie drückst du deine Meinung aus/ Wie bittest du um etwas?**
>
> Folgende Redewendungen helfen dir, eine bestimmte Absicht auszudrücken:
> - Wenn du eine **eigene Meinung** ausdrücken willst:
>   In my opinion, …
>   I think (that) …
>   I believe (that) …
>   I guess (that) … (eher vermutend)
>
> - Wenn du um **Auskunft** bitten willst:
>   Could you tell me …, please?
>   Can you tell me …, please?
>
> - Wenn du um **Zusendung** bitten willst:
>   Could you send me …, please?
>
> - Wenn du um **Erklärung** bitten willst:
>   Could you explain it to me, please?
>
> - Wenn du um **Antwort** bitten willst:
>   Could you please answer my letter?
>
> - Wenn du um **Entschuldigung** bitten willst:
>   I'm sorry (that) …

Could you tell me the way to the Notting Hill Carnival, please?

9 What do you say in the following situations?

a Sage, dass deiner Meinung nach *Notting Hill* der schönste Liebesfilm ist.

_____

b Deine Gasteltern bitten dich, Ihnen von dem Film zu erzählen.

_____

c Frage, ob deine Gasteltern den Kölner Karneval kennen.

_____

d Sage, dass deiner Meinung nach der Kölner Karneval die großartigste
Straßenparty in Deutschland ist.

_____

10 E-Mail

Sieh dir das Poster genau an und schreibe dann eine E-Mail, die mindestens
10 Sätze umfasst. Denke an den Aufbau einer E-Mail und halte dich an unten
stehende Angaben:

Anne und ihr Bruder Mark sind 15 und 17 Jahre alt. Die Geschwister leben in
London und haben dir in ihrer letzten Mail kurz vom Notting Hill Carnival be-
richtet, dir Fotos davon geschickt und dich zu einem einwöchigen Besuch
Ende August eingeladen.

- Bedanke dich für ihre E-Mail und die Einladung nach London.
- Sage, dass du gerne nach London kommen würdest, um sie zu besuchen.

- Berichte, dass du vor einem Jahr schon einmal mit deinen Eltern eine Woche in London verbracht hast, und dass es dir dort sehr gut gefallen hat.
- Sage, dass ihr eine Stadtrundfahrt mit einem Doppeldeckerbus gemacht habt. Berichte, dass du Buckingham Palace, den Tower und die St. Paul's Cathedral gesehen hast, aber noch nie in Notting Hill warst.
- Frage, wie oft die beiden schon beim Notting Hill Carnival waren.
- Sage, dass du nicht viel darüber weißt. Frage, woher die Teilnehmer*innen und Zuschauer*innen beim Notting Hill Carnival kommen. Frage, was Anne und Mark am Carnival am liebsten mögen.
- Erkundige dich, welche Kleidung die Zuschauer*innen beim Carnival tragen und wie die Speisen sind.
- Erkläre, dass du überrascht bist, dass es in London so eine Veranstaltung gibt, und frage, woher der Notting Hill Carnival ursprünglich kommt.
- Ergänze noch, dass es großartig wäre, wenn Anne und Mark dir noch einen Link zum Notting Hill Carnival senden könnten.

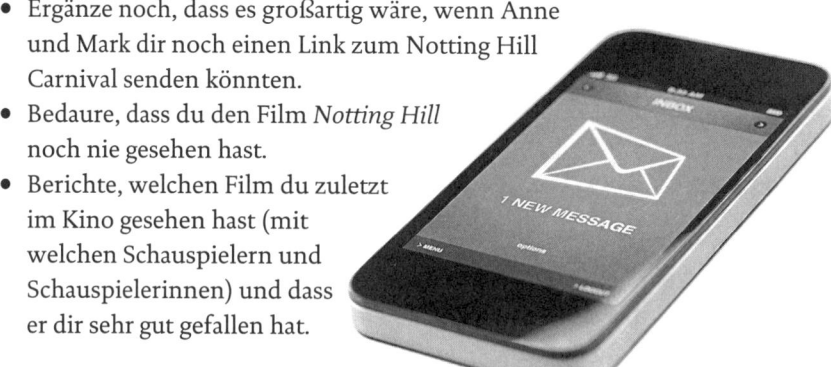

- Bedaure, dass du den Film *Notting Hill* noch nie gesehen hast.
- Berichte, welchen Film du zuletzt im Kino gesehen hast (mit welchen Schauspielern und Schauspielerinnen) und dass er dir sehr gut gefallen hat.

Topic 2: Global Warming

1 The world's atmosphere is getting warmer and warmer. This is the 'greenhouse effect'. It means that gases like carbon dioxide keep heat in the atmosphere. That will change the world
5 this century.

Europe will be a warmer place in future with drier summers and longer periods without rain. 'What's wrong with that?' you can ask. Well, there will be much wetter autumns and winters.
10 In other words there will be more flooding.

In Russia there is the problem of the melting 'permafrost'. 'Permafrost' is ground which is frozen all the year round and covers 65 % of the country. People build houses on it and keep food frozen in holes in the ground. But global warming means that the permafrost is melting.
15 Experts say that in 25 years it will move back 250 kilometres. Houses will fall down, railway lines will sink and roads will disappear. This has already started and will get much worse.

In the USA the horror movie fantasy of the sea covering the cities on the east coast is much closer to happening. With global warming temperatures
20 will rise by as much as 6 °C. This will make the sea expand and rise by up to 60 cm. Now add storms and bad weather and cities like New York and Boston will be in trouble from floods. The other effect of global warming will be the spread of dangerous diseases. Doctors have found malaria for the first time ever in New York and higher temperatures will allow insects like mosquitoes
25 to spread disease easily.

Britain produces as much carbon dioxide as the whole of Africa. But Africa will also pay the price for global warming. The future for Africa is bad because there will be more floods and more food shortages. Diseases like malaria will also spread to new areas.
30 The people of Japan live with volcanoes, earthquakes, typhoons and tidal waves. But global warming will be much worse. It will make 15 000 000 people leave their homes! Most of the Japanese population live on the coast between Tokyo and Osaka, and in Tokyo itself millions live below sea level. Health problems will also increase along with the rising temperatures.

Adapted from 'Welcome to the new world', The Guardian, Nov 14, 2000

Vocabulary

greenhouse effect (line 2): *Treibhauseffekt*
carbon dioxide (line 3): CO_2 *(Kohlendioxid)*
flooding (line 10): *Überflutung*
to melt (line 11): *schmelzen*
ground (line 12): *Erdboden*
to cover (line 13): *bedecken*
to disappear (line 16): *verschwinden*
to expand (line 20): *sich ausweiten*
to rise, rose, risen (*irregular verb*, line 20): *sich erheben, ansteigen*
to spread (line 23): *sich ausbreiten*
disease (line 23): *Krankheit*
food shortage (line 28): *Nahrungsmittelmangel*
tidal waves (line 30/31): *Springfluten*

Working on the text

11 Tick (✓) the right answer.

    a The 'greenhouse effect' means that in winter the weather in Europe will be …

      ☐ drier.
      ☐ colder.
      ☐ the same.
      ☐ wetter.

    b The area of ground which has permafrost in Russia is …

      ☐ less than half the country.
      ☐ getting smaller.
      ☐ 250 kilometres wide.
      ☐ getting bigger.

    c Permafrost is useful because you can …

      ☐ store food in it.
      ☐ grow food in it.
      ☐ cook food in it.
      ☐ find food in it.

d In the USA the idea that the sea will cover the east coast cities is …

- ☐ a horror movie.
- ☐ getting warmer.
- ☐ getting much more likely.
- ☐ rising.

e Global warming will create …

- ☐ new diseases.
- ☐ the spread of diseases.
- ☐ fewer diseases.
- ☐ diseases which kill mosquitoes.

f In Japan global warming will …

- ☐ cause earthquakes.
- ☐ make volcanoes erupt.
- ☐ cause tidal waves.
- ☐ make the sea rise.

g In Japan global warming will …

- ☐ make millions of people homeless.
- ☐ make life in Tokyo and Osaka easier.
- ☐ get millions of people to live below sea level.
- ☐ make life for people much better.

12 True or false? Tick (✓) the right answer.

		true	false
a	There'll be more flooding all over Europe because of global warming.	☐	☐
b	More than half of the ground in Russia is covered by 'permafrost'.	☐	☐
c	The 'permafrost' in Russia hasn't started to melt yet.	☐	☐
d	In the USA the greenhouse effect will make the sea expand and change the climate.	☐	☐
e	The spread of diseases will be another effect of rising temperatures all over the world.	☐	☐
f	Africa produces more CO_2 than Great Britain.	☐	☐
g	Only a few people in Japan live below sea level, so global warming won't have effects on them.	☐	☐

13 Complete the table with examples of the effects of global warming.

Europe	Russia: melting 'permafrost'	Africa
wetter _____ and winters	_____ will fall down	more _____ shortages
drier _____	the _____ will melt	more _____
longer periods without _____	roads will _____	malaria will spread to new _____

Language

14 Translate the underlined words into German.

The greenhouse effect means that gases like CO_2 keep <u>heat</u> (a) in the atmosphere. That will <u>change</u> (b) the world's climate this <u>century</u> (c). All over the world there will be more <u>flooding</u> (d). <u>Areas</u> (e) along the coasts will be flooded. The global warming will make many people <u>leave</u> (f) their homes. <u>Health problems</u> (g) will also <u>increase</u> (h).

a *Hitze* _____   b _____

c _____   d _____

e _____   f _____

g _____   h _____

15 Fill in the gaps.

noun	adjective
danger	*dangerous*
health	
	warm
	long

16 Fill in the gaps. Find the opposite of the words underlined.

a a <u>short</u> distance   →   a _long_ distance

b <u>above</u> sea level   →   _____ sea level

c _____ weather   →   <u>fine</u> weather

d the <u>first</u> time   →   the _____ time

e _____ temperatures   →   <u>high</u> temperatures

f an <u>easy</u> question   →   a _____ question

g a(n) _____ problem   →   a <u>local</u> problem

h <u>ask</u> a question   →   _____ a question

i _____ weather   →   <u>wet</u> weather

17 Give three examples for each collective noun.

a buildings: _houses_   _skyscrapers_   _towers_

b continents: _____   _____   _____

c weather conditions: _____   _____   _____

d natural catastrophes: _____   _____   _____

18 Cross out the word that doesn't fit.

a volcanoes, earthquakes, typhoons, ~~coasts~~

b Europe, New York, Boston, Tokyo

c storms, floods, temperatures, typhoons

d atmosphere, gas, CO_2, century

19 Which word **sounds** different at the underlined part?

a ch<u>i</u>ld – unt<u>i</u>l – w<u>i</u>ld – n<u>i</u>ght – r<u>i</u>de   _until_

b k<u>ee</u>p – h<u>ea</u>t – p<u>eo</u>ple – dis<u>ea</u>se – h<u>ea</u>lth – m<u>ea</u>n   _____

c c<u>oa</u>st – cl<u>o</u>se – fl<u>oo</u>d – als<u>o</u> – r<u>oa</u>ds – wh<u>o</u>le   _____

d r<u>i</u>se – l<u>i</u>ke – dr<u>y</u> – pr<u>i</u>ce – <u>i</u>nsects – railway l<u>i</u>nes   _____

e c<u>ou</u>ntry – all<u>ow</u> – d<u>ow</u>n – r<u>ou</u>nd – h<u>ou</u>ses – f<u>ou</u>nd   _____

20 Put the words in the right order to make sentences about global warming.

a Der Treibhauseffekt wird die Welt verändern.
the / change / the / world / will / 'greenhouse effect'

_____

b In Europa wird es mehr Überflutungen geben.
there / in / be / will / more / Europe / flooding

_____

c Sogar in den USA werden sich Krankheiten ausbreiten.
even / USA / the / in / will / diseases / spread

_____

d In Afrika wird es mehr Nahrungsmittelmangel geben.
there / more / Africa / food shortage / be / in / will

_____

e In Japan werden Millionen von Menschen ihre Heimat verlassen.
in / will / millions / their / people / homes / Japan / of / leave

_____

f Gesundheitliche Probleme werden auf der ganzen Welt zunehmen.
health problems / world / will / over / the / increase / all

_____

21 Ask questions. Choose the correct word for each sentence:
when – where – what – why – who – how many

a _____ are there many volcanoes? – In Japan.

b _____ people live under sea level in Tokyo? – Millions!

c _____ is the global warming dangerous for Africa? – Because there will be more floods, more food shortage and more diseases.

d _____ produces as much CO_2 as the whole of Africa? – Britain.

Grammar

Will-future – Die Zukunft mit will

Zukünftige Geschehnisse werden im Englischen mit dem **will-future** ausgedrückt:
Mit dem *will-future* macht man **Vorhersagen für die Zukunft**. *Will* steht oft nach
Ausdrücken wie *I think, I'm sure.*
Beispiel: I'm sure Peter <u>will help</u> you.

Wie bildest du das *will-future*?

● Das *will-future* bildest du mit *will* + Grundform.

> I
> He/She/It   **will play**.
> We/You/They

In der Umgangssprache wird *will* häufig zu *'ll* verkürzt.
Beispiel: <u>I'll</u> come.

● Die **Verneinung** des *will-future* bildest du mit *will not* + Grundform.
Will not wird meistens zu **won't** verkürzt.
Beispiel: It <u>won't be</u> sunny at the weekend.

● **Fragen** im *will-future* bildest du mit *will* + Subjekt + Grundform.
Beispiel: <u>Will you write</u> me an e-mail with your address?

22 Weather forecast
Complete the weather forecast.

Tomorrow it _____ in
Scotland with _____ and
_____ winds. In the Midlands
it _____ mainly _____ with
light _____. In the south of Great
Britain it _____
with _____.

23

Sandra's party

Fill in the gaps

will take – will wait – will have – will use – will get – will bring – will come

a If Sandra's parents let her, she _____ a party.

b If her Dad allows it, Sandra _____ her father's car to go shopping for her party.

c She hopes nobody _____ alcoholic drinks to her party.

d Sandra hopes a lot of people from her class _____ to the party.

e If it rains, they _____ the bus.

f If John promises not to come late, they _____ for him.

g John's sister _____ very angry, if she sees him eating all her chocolates at the party.

Text Production

24 E-Mail

Beachte: Deine E-Mail sollte mindestens 10 Sätze umfassen.

Denke an den Aufbau einer E-Mail.

Angaben zum Adressaten: Dein Freund Thomas (14) aus Edinburgh hat dich eingeladen ihn zu besuchen.

- Bedanke dich für seine lange E-Mail und die Einladung nach Edinburgh.
- Schreibe, dass du ihn so bald wie möglich besuchen wirst. Du wirst eine Freundin/ einen Freund mitbringen. Ihr werdet anfangen, Geld für den Flug zu sparen.
- Berichte, dass du in der Schule an einem Projekt mitarbeiten wirst: Du wirst dich im Internet über den Treibhauseffekt genauer informieren und für deine Klasse ein Plakat gestalten.
- Erkläre, was der Treibhauseffekt ist, und beschreibe, wie sich das Klima in Europa in Zukunft verändern wird (im Sommer, im Herbst).
- Sage, dass es überall auf der Welt wahrscheinlich häufiger zu Überschwemmungen kommen wird.
- Frage, ob auch Thomas in der Schule über die Folgen des Treibhauseffektes sprechen wird.
- Sage, dass du vermutest, dass die Menschen die globale Erwärmung der Atmosphäre in Zukunft nicht aufhalten werden können.
- Drücke aber die Hoffnung aus, dass Ärzte und Ärztinnen die Ausbreitung von Krankheiten stoppen werden.
- Drücke die Hoffnung aus, dass Thomas bald zurückschreiben wird.
- Bitte ihn auch, seine Eltern zu grüßen.

Topic 3: Beef in Fries?

1 Hindus believe cows to be holy. It would be as unthinkable for them to eat beef, as it would be for a cowboy to eat his own horse. Harish Barti, a Hindu living in America, said, 'Eating a cow for a Hindu would be like eating your mother herself.' Like him many Hindus living in the USA have problems in
5 mixing their religious habits with the American lifestyle …

Mr Sharma, a Hindu working for Boeing in Seattle, says that before 1990 he never went to a McDonald's restaurant. He didn't eat hamburgers or cheese-burgers as they are made of beef and he didn't eat French fried potatoes there as they were cooked in beef fat.

10 But in 1990 McDonald's switched from beef fat to "100 % vegetable oil" to cook its French fries. Now Mr Sharma, like thousands of Hindu Americans, began going to McDonald's to eat what they believed were vegetarian fries.

In April 1990 he was shocked when he opened his India West newspaper and read **'Where's the Beef? It's in your French Fries.'** The newspaper said that
15 McDonald's French Fries are seasoned in the factory with beef flavour before they are sent to the restaurants and cooked in vegetable oil.

Mr Sharma was shocked about the fact that he had eaten 'beef in fries'. 'The mistake wasn't mine,' Mr Sharma says. 'It was theirs. They didn't tell the truth. I can't blame myself.'

20 Now Mr Sharma is representing the Hindus and vegetarians of America in a lawsuit that accuses McDonald's of deliberately misleading its customers.

'The fault isn't ours,' Walt Riker, a spokesman for McDonald's said in an interview last week. 'We certainly don't market ourselves as vegetarian.'

At the Anand Bhavan Vegetarian restaurant in Houston, Mahendra Jagirdar,
25 an engineer, said he had stopped eating at McDonald's when he heard about the fries. 'I'm a pretty strict vegetarian myself. You can choose: you can eat at vegetarian restaurants or you can go to McDonald's.'

As for Mr Sharma, he is looking for ways to clean himself.

'I am now planning to go to India to swim in the holy river
30 Ganges. It will make things better, but the damage is already done.'

Vocabulary

beef (heading): *Rindfleisch*
fries (heading): *eigentlich* French fried potatoes: *Pommes frites*
holy (line 1): *heilig*
unthinkable (line 1): *unvorstellbar, undenkbar*
religious habits (line 5): *religiöse Gewohnheiten*
to switch (line 10): *hier: (Produktion) umstellen*
beef flavour (line 15): *Rindfleischaroma, Rindfleischgeschmack*
seasoned (line 15): *mit Würze, gewürzt*
to blame someone (line 19): *jemandem die Schuld geben, jemanden verant-wortlich machen*
to represent s.o. (line 20): *hier: jemanden vertreten*
lawsuit (line 21): *Rechtsstreit, (Zivil-)Prozess*
deliberate (line 21): *bewusst, absichtlich*
to mislead someone, misled, misled (*irregular verb*, line 21): *jemanden täuschen, irreführen*
to accuse someone (line 21): *jemanden anklagen*

Working on the text

25 Tick (✓) the right answer.

a Hindus in America …

☐ don't have any problems with food.
☐ like to eat steaks.
☐ like to eat horses.
☐ are not allowed to eat beef.

b Before 1990 Mr Sharma …

☐ often went to a McDonald's restaurant.
☐ ate hamburgers.
☐ ate cheeseburgers.
☐ didn't eat at Mc Donald's.

c After 1990 Mr Sharma began to eat McDonald's French fries because …

☐ he believed they were vegetarian.
☐ he had enough money.
☐ he liked the taste of the oil.
☐ everyone else did.

d   McDonald's . . .

☐ cooked their French fries in beef fat.

☐ cooked their French fries in the factory.

☐ used beef fat and vegetable oil to cook French fries.

☐ flavoured French fries with beef in the factory.

e   Mr Sharma said that the mistake was . . .

☐ a friend's.

☐ his.

☐ McDonald's.

☐ no-one's.

f   Walt Riker said that the fault was . . .

☐ McDonald's.

☐ the vegetarian restaurant's.

☐ not McDonald's.

☐ the market's.

g   When Mahendra Jagirdar heard about the fries he . . .

☐ stopped going to McDonald's.

☐ became a vegetarian.

☐ went to India.

☐ became an engineer.

26   You know a lot about Mr Sharma. Fill in the gaps.

a   Mr Sharma is a _____.

b   He _____ for Boeing in Seattle.

c   He never went _____ before 1990.

d   He began going to McDonald's to eat _____.

e   He was _____ when he read the news about beef in fries.

f   He accuses McDonald's of misleading _____.

g   He is looking for ways to _____.

27 Match the beginnings and endings. There is one extra ending.

A Mc Donald's switched   (1) its French fries with beef flavour.

B The fast-food chain seasoned   (2) their customers.

C McDonald's restaurants misled   (3) from beef fat to vegetable oil.

D Mr Sharma is representing   (4) French fries in 100 % vegetable oil.

                                           (5) the Hindus of America.

A	B	C	D

Language

28 Put one of the following words in each space in the sentences below:
to – at – in – of – for – by – in front of   on – up – to – out.

a I like to eat _____.

b Do you like to go _____
fast-food restaurants?

c Do you prefer a simple café
_____ a big restaurant?

d I'm very fond _____
Italian food.

e I hate to wash _____
the dishes. Let's leave the kitchen!

f Shall we call a taxi or go
_____ tube?

g I'm hungry. What's _____
the menu today?

h Can you ask _____ the menu, please?

i Oh, look, the menu is lying over there _____ the mirror.
I can get it myself.

j I looked _____ the menu and found some vegetarian dishes.

k Would you put the menu _____ the cupboard, please?

Menu

Steak and Mushroom Pie ..	£ 8.95
Fish Pie	£ 8.95
Lamb and Apricot Pie	£ 8.95
Cumberland Pie	£ 8.95
Fish and Chips	£ 8.95
Roast Chicken	£ 9.95
Beef Stew	£ 8.95
English Lamb Steak	£ 9.95
Smoked Haddock	£ 9.95

29 Classifications:

Mercury, Mars, Venus	p _l a n e t s_
Buddhism, Hinduism, Christianity	r _ _ _ _ _ _ _
Australia, Asia, Europe	c _ _ _ _ _ _ _ _
Atlantic, Pacific, Indian	o _ _ _ _ _
Swiss, American, Italian	n _ _ _ _ _ _ _ _ _ _
lipstick, mascara, eye-liner	m _ _ _ - _ _
penicillin, morphine, codeine	d _ _ _ _

30 Who is the boss? Match the items on the left with the 'boss' on the right.

TV programme	captain
restaurant	headteacher
school	foreperson
football team	manager
group of workers	choir leader
company	producer
choir	shop keeper
pet shop	managing director

31 The Sharmas are moving. There are a lot of things left in the mover's van to carry into the house. Match the objects and their translation.

A blanket	(1) Vorhang, Gardine
B carpet	(2) Kissen
C bookshelf	(3) Hocker
D curtain	(4) Decke
E desk	(5) Teppich
F cushion	(6) Bücherregal
G stool	(7) Schreibtisch

A	B	C	D	E	F	G

Grammar

> **Personal** and *possessive pronouns* – persönliche und besitzanzeigende Fürwörter
> **Persönliche Fürwörter** stehen für Personen oder Dinge. Mit den **besitzanzeigenden Fürwörtern** sagt man, was jemandem **gehört**.

persönliches Fürwort	besitzanzeigendes Fürwort (mit Substantiv)	besitzanzeigendes Fürwort (ohne Substantiv)
I	my car	mine
you	your car	yours
he	his car	his
she	her car	hers
it	its car	its
we	our car	ours
you	your car	yours
they	their car	theirs

Beispiel: I'm looking for the dictionary. Whose is it? – It's <u>my</u> dictionary. It's <u>mine</u>.
Look at this skateboard. Is it y<u>ours</u>? – No, ask Sharon, I think it's <u>hers</u>.
Our neighbours' flat is as big as <u>ours</u>. But our garden is bigger than <u>theirs</u>.

32 Whose is it: mine – yours – his – hers – ours – theirs?
Before the final tests Mr White, the teacher, is giving the students
their lost property back.

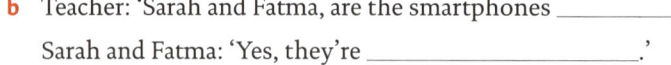

a Teacher: 'Susie, are these headphones _____?'
   Susie: 'Yes, they're _____.'

b Teacher: 'Sarah and Fatma, are the smartphones _____?'
   Sarah and Fatma: 'Yes, they're _____.'

c Teacher: 'Robert says it is _____.
   Is that true?'
   John: 'No, it is Peggy's ball. Yes, I'm sure the basketball is
   _____.'

d Teacher: 'Where are Liz and Peter? Here are two exercise books.'
   John: 'They're at the gym. But I know the exercise books are
   _____. Look at the names.'

e John: 'I've found a bag of sweets. Is it _____?'

Michael: 'No, ask the girls. Perhaps it's _____.'

John: 'OK, but if nobody owns it, the bag of sweets is _____!'

f John: 'Mr White, I've found these old trainers.

Are they _____?'

Teacher: 'Let me see – Yes, of course they're _____!'

Reflexive pronouns – rückbezügliche Fürwörter

- Die **rückbezüglichen Fürwörter** werden so genannt, weil sie sich auf das Subjekt des Satzes beziehen. Im Englischen gibt es folgende **Formen:**

I		myself	
You		yourself	
He/She/It	hurt	himself/herself/itself	seriously.
We		ourselves	
You		yourselves	
They		themselves	

Beispiele: I hurt <u>myself</u> yesterday, I broke my leg.
<u>We</u> enjoyed <u>ourselves</u> at the circus.
Tommy, be careful with that knife, <u>you</u> could hurt <u>yourself</u>!

- Mit den rückbezüglichen Fürwörtern kann man auch sagen, dass eine **Handlung ohne fremde Hilfe selbst vollzogen** wurde:
Beispiele: Nobody helped me. I cooked the meal <u>myself</u>.
She's teaching <u>herself</u> a new computer programme.

---

33 Choose the correct pronoun.

The Sharmas' new home

Mr Sharma and ___*his*___ family moved to a new house because they had to leave _____ apartment. Asif and _____ little brother got a big room on the first floor.

_____ decorated the room _____. 'Can you help _____ to carry the computer upstairs?' the boys asked

Mr Sharma. 'Oh, you don't need _____, it isn't heavy, you can carry it _____!' he answered.

'Here are some computer games, Asif. Are they _____?' Mr Sharma asked. 'Yes, they're _____,' _____ son answered.

'Have a break! Would _____ like a piece of cheesecake?' Mrs Sharma asked. 'I prepared it _____ in _____ new oven.'

'Great, I love cheesecake,' Asif answered, ran into the kitchen and took the sharp knife carelessly. He tried to cut the cake and hurt _____.

_____ mother got some plaster from _____ handbag and put it round _____ bleeding finger. Poor Asif.

Now they all have tea and cheesecake. '_____ new home is great. We'll enjoy _____ here, I'm sure, as we have more room for _____ all now.'

Text Production

34 Wandzeitung für Mitschüler*innen:
'It's your body – get fit and check your diet!'

Beachte: Zeige erst das falsche Verhalten der meisten Jugendlichen und fordere dann zum Nachdenken über den eigenen Körper auf.

Achte auf die richtige Darstellung (als Aufforderung, auch in Stichpunkten), damit alle, die die Wandzeitung lesen, motiviert werden, sich gesünder zu ernähren und Sport zu treiben. Lade die Leser*innen in den Jugendklub ein, wo verschiedene Aktivitäten angeboten werden.

- Beschreibe das Fehlverhalten der Jugendlichen so:
  Heutzutage haben viele Jugendliche einen ungesunden Lebensstil.
  Jugendliche essen oft ungesunde Lebensmittel.
  Sie essen in Eile, im Stehen in einem Fast-Food-Restaurant.
  Sie essen zu viel *junk food* mit sehr viel Fett und Zucker.
  Sie sind nicht aktiv in ihrer Freizeit.
  Sie treiben nicht viel Sport.

- Frage den Leser/die Leserin, wie er/sie fit bleibt: Frage, ob er/sie Sport treibt oder lieber fernsieht, im Internet surft oder Videospiele spielt.
- Erkläre, welche Hobbys du hast.
  Sage, welche Sportart du ausübst und wie häufig.
  Sage, wo du deinen Sport treibst, dein Hobby pflegst.
- Frage den Leser/die Leserin, ob er/sie dies jemals versucht hat:
  Badminton spielen, Klettern, Jogging, Judo.
- Rufe den Leser/die Leserin dazu auf, in das Jugendzentrum zu kommen:
  Erkläre, dass man hier aktive junge Leute trifft.
  Erwähne, dass man in Kochkursen viel über gesunde Ernährung und das Kochen lernt.
- Rufe dazu auf mehr Sport zu treiben, auf die Ernährung zu achten und fit und aktiv zu bleiben
- Weise darauf hin, dass es um den eigenen Körper geht, dass man auf sich selbst aufpassen soll.

Topic 4: Star Problem

Each week we focus on a problem that a star has met and overcome. This week Pete Jones of TV's 'Young Sports Stars' talks about bullying:

1 'The first time someone bullied me was when I was in Year 9 at school. Almost overnight everyone in the class started calling me names and teasing me.

5 I think it was because I was on TV in "Young Sports Stars". I think they were jealous of me or something. I never really found out why they decided to bully me. They just did.

They did things to me in the classroom and out of school, and even during my exams. What really shocked me was that some of the bullies were my

10 friends. The more I was on TV, the more they bullied me. It went on for months and months and got worse and worse. I felt terrible. I didn't want to go to school any more.

Then I told my mum and my teacher. My teacher took me to see the Head. The Head put me in a room next to hers, so that I didn't have to mix with the

15 bullies. I didn't want to leave my class, but being on my own helped. Soon the bullies forgot about me and I moved back into my class again about six weeks before the summer holiday. When school started again in September no-one bullied me. I'm so glad that I talked to my mum and my teacher. Talking made things better. I'm OK now but some of the other guys on "Young Sports Stars"

20 also had problems with bullying. Bullies hurt one of them really badly. So you can see that bullying can happen to anyone.'

Adapted from 'Star Problem', Live and Kicking, Issue 86, Nov 2000, p. 37

Vocabulary

to bully (introduction): *terrorisieren, mobben*
to tease (line 4): *ärgern*
jealous (line 6): *eifersüchtig*
the Head (line 13): *Rektor*in*

Working on the text

35 Tick (✓) the right answer.

a Pete thinks the class bullied him because ...

☐ of his name.

☐ he was on TV.

☐ he was good at sport.

☐ he was in Year 9.

b Pete ...

☐ never found out exactly why the class decided to bully him.

☐ knew exactly why the class decided to bully him.

☐ didn't know the names of the bullies.

☐ was jealous of the other people in the class.

c The class bullied Pete ...

☐ when he was on TV.

☐ only when he was at school.

☐ only out of school.

☐ at school, out of school and during exams.

d Because of the bullying Pete ...

☐ didn't want to go to school any more.

☐ found that his schoolwork got worse and worse.

☐ was on TV more often.

☐ made some new friends.

e After Pete saw the Head ...

☐ he felt terrible.

☐ he went to another school.

☐ he studied in a room on his own.

☐ he was in a room next to his mother.

f When school began again after the summer holiday ...

☐ everyone bullied Pete.

☐ no-one bullied Pete.

☐ his mum and teacher talked to Pete.

☐ no-one talked to Pete.

g Pete thinks that bullying ...

☐ happens to everyone.

☐ only happens to people who are on TV.

☐ happens to people who talk to the teacher.

☐ can happen to anyone.

36 True or false? Correct the false sentences (3).

	true	false
a Pete was a bully.	☐	☐
b No-one in Pete's class called him names.	☐	☐
c The bullying started suddenly.	☐	☐
d Pete was really surprised that some of the bullies were his friends.	☐	☐
e Pete's mother took him to see the Head.	☐	☐
f Pete didn't have to spend time with the rest of his class.	☐	☐
g Other people on the same TV show had problems like Pete's.	☐	☐

37 Fill in the gaps. Write correct sentences about Pete's problems.

a   Almost overnight everyone in the class ___*started bullying*___ Pete.

b   The bullies were _____ of Pete being on TV.

c   Pete was shocked that some of the bullies _____ his friends.

d   The more Pete was on TV the _____ they bullied him.

e   Pete never _____ why they decided to bully him.

f   He felt glad that he _____ his mum and teacher.

g   Talking _____ with his problems.

38 Find a sentence with almost the same meaning. Tick (✓) the right answer.

a   Some other students who were on TV also had problems with bullying. Bullies hurt one of them really badly.

☐ One of them was badly injured.

☐ Bullies hurt themselves really badly.

☐ A student on 'Young Sports Stars' hurt himself.

b   Pete: 'I didn't want to leave my class, but being on my own helped.'

☐ It was good to be home again.

☐ It helped that I didn't have to mix with the bullies.

☐ It helped to be with the bullies for months and months.

c   Pete: 'Talking made things better.'

☐ Talking won't help you.

☐ It helps to tell other people about your problems.

☐ Never talk too much about other people.

d   Pete: 'You can see that bullying can happen to anyone.'

☐ Everybody can be bullied.

☐ Only some students are bullied.

☐ Bullying can't happen to anyone.

Language

39 Name one thing in each sentence. Pete learned a lot at school:

a   In social studies they learned about ___*political conflicts*___.

b   In geography he learned about _____.

c   In history he learned about _____.

d   In biology he learned about _____.

e   In mathematics he learned about _____.

40 Odd one out: Which is not a kind of TV programme?

a   love story / game show / soap / newspaper

b   cartoon / action film / magazine / talk show

c   mobile / news / comedy / science fiction

d   horror film / sports report / documentary / picture book

41 Put the words in the correct list.
a mess – the bed – a mistake – divorced – a job – a secret – tea or coffee – someone waiting – angry – a promise – married – dressed – quiet

get ...	make ...	keep ...
... divorced	... a mess	... a promise

Grammar

Simple past – Die 1. Vergangenheit

Das *simple past* verwendest du,

- um in der Vergangenheit **abgeschlossene Handlungen / Ereignisse** auszudrücken,
  Beispiel: Last year I <u>spent</u> my holidays in Italy.

- um Handlungen/Ereignisse auszudrücken, die **in der Vergangenheit aufeinander folgten**.
  Beispiel: He <u>walked</u> into the room and <u>closed</u> the door.

- um **Handlungen** auszudrücken, **die sich in der Vergangenheit wiederholten**.
  Beispiel: When he was a child, his mother <u>told</u> him bed-time stories every night.

Das *simple past* steht häufig nach Wörtern wie *yesterday, last night, three weeks ago, last year, in 2007*, etc.

Wie bildest du das *simple past*?

- Bei **regelmäßigen Verben** fügst du meist die **Endung -ed an die Grundform** an.
  Beispiel: help   ➞   help<u>ed</u>
  Es gibt einige Ausnahmen in der Schreibweise:

  - Nach kurzem betontem Vokal wird der **Endkonsonant verdoppelt**.
    Beispiel: stop   ➞   stopp<u>ed</u>

  - Nach einem Konsonanten wird aus einem **-y am Wortende ein -i-**.
    Beispiel: cry   ➞   cri<u>ed</u>

  - Wenn der letzte Buchstabe ein *-e* ist, wird **nur -d angefügt**.
    Beispiel: arriv<u>e</u>   ➞   arrive<u>d</u>

- **Unregelmäßige Verben** haben unregelmäßige Vergangenheitsformen. Diese musst du **auswendig lernen**. Siehe dazu S. 112 f.
  Beispiel: meet   ➞   <u>met</u>

- Die **Verneinung** im *simple past* bildest du mit *didn't* + Grundform.
  Beispiel: Pete <u>didn't want</u> to go to school any more.

- **Fragen** im *simple past* bildest du mithilfe des Frageworts *did/didn't* + Grundform.
  Beispiel: <u>Did</u> they <u>bully</u> him because he was on TV in 'Young Sports Stars'?
               <u>Didn't</u> they <u>stop</u> bullying Pete after a while?

Beachte: **to be** (sein) verändert sich im **simple past**.

	Singular		Plural	
bejahter Aussagesatz	I	was happy.	We	
	You	were happy.	You	were happy.
	He/she/it	was happy.	They	
verneinter Aussagesatz	I	wasn't happy.	We	
	You	weren't happy.	You	weren't happy.
	He/she/it	wasn't happy.	They	
Frage	Was	I happy?		we happy?
	Were	you happy?	Were	you happy?
	Was	he/she/it happy?		They happy?

42 Fill in the correct verb in the past tense:
can – bully – feel – put – to be – tell – make – write – start
Pete's story:

a Last year even my friends _____ me at school.

b I _____ very shocked.

c So I _____ my mother and my teacher.

d Talking _____ things better.

e I _____ terrible being bullied.

43 Complete these sentences. Use the simple past tense.

a Pete ___was___ (to be) in 'Young Sports Stars' when they ___bullied___ (bully) him at school.

b It _____ (shock) Pete that some of the bullies _____ (to be) his friends.

c The bullying _____ (go on) for months and it _____ (get) worse.

d He _____ (not want) to leave his class.

e The Head _____ (put) him in a room next to hers.

f It _____ (help) Pete being on his own.

g The bullies _____ (forget) Pete after the summer holidays.

44 Pete's diary

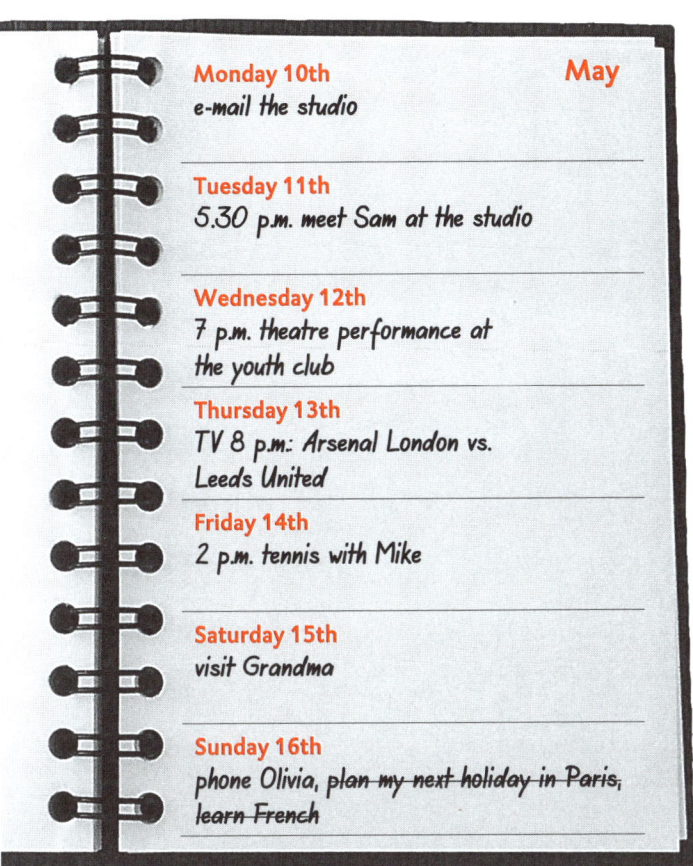

> **Monday 10th**   **May**
> e-mail the studio
>
> ──────────────────────
>
> **Tuesday 11th**
> 5.30 p.m. meet Sam at the studio
>
> ──────────────────────
>
> **Wednesday 12th**
> 7 p.m. theatre performance at
> the youth club
>
> **Thursday 13th**
> TV 8 p.m.: Arsenal London vs.
> Leeds United
>
> **Friday 14th**
> 2 p.m. tennis with Mike
>
> ──────────────────────
>
> **Saturday 15th**
> visit Grandma
>
> ──────────────────────
>
> **Sunday 16th**
> phone Olivia, ~~plan my next holiday in Paris,~~
> ~~learn French~~

Report what Pete did last week:

On Monday Pete __e-mailed the studio_____.

On Tuesday he _____.

On Wednesday he _____.

On Thursday he _____.

On Friday he _____.

On Saturday he _____.

On Sunday he _____ but he _____ or

_____.

45 Busy Pete! His grandmother is ill and she can't do things herself. Here's what Pete did yesterday.

'Yesterday I had a lot to do:

First I _____ a meal for her.

Then I _____ the shopping.

I _____ milk, tea and bread.

Grandma _____ till 3 o'clock.

I _____ the flowers.

Afterwards I _____ to repair
Grandma's TV set …

… but I _____ do it.
I hope Grandma will be OK, soon.'

Text Production

Sprachliche Mittel: Wie drückst du Gefühle aus?

- Wenn du **Vorlieben / Abneigung** ausdrücken willst:

  I like …   I can't stand …
  I love …   I hate …
  I enjoy …   I dislike …

- Wenn du **Bedauern, Mitleid** ausdrücken willst:

  I'm (very) sorry …
  I regret (that) …

- Wenn du **Enttäuschung ausdrücken** willst:

  What a pity!
  I'm very disappointed …
  I'm very sad …

- Wenn du **Hoffnung, gute Wünsche** ausdrücken willst:

  I hope (it'll …)   Best wishes …
  I'm sure (it'll …)   I wish you all the best …

- Wenn du **Gleichgültigkeit / Unentschiedenheit** ausdrücken willst:

  I don't mind …
  I don't care about …

46 What do you say in the following situations?

    a Sage, dass du Talkshows im Fernsehen nicht magst.

    _____

    b Sage, dass es dir nichts ausmacht, wenn dich jemand ärgert.

    _____

    c Sage, dass du es nicht ausstehen kannst, wenn jemand einen
       Mitschüler/eine Mitschülerin terrorisiert.

    _____

    d Drücke die Hoffnung aus, dass dein Gesprächspartner/deine
       Gesprächspartnerin die Konflikte bald lösen wird.

    _____

    e Wünsche ihm/ihr alles Gute.

    _____

47 E-Mail
Beachte: Deine E-Mail sollte mindestens 10 Sätze umfassen.
Denke an die richtige Form und achte auf die richtige Zeit.

Angaben zur Adressatin: Deine Freundin
Alice (14) aus London hat dir ihre Situation
in der Schule beschrieben:
Seit sie vor drei Monaten bei einer Quiz-Show
im Fernsehen viel Geld gewann,
tyrannisierten ihre Mitschüler sie,
sogar ihre besten Freundinnen.

- Bedanke dich für ihre lange E-Mail und die Einladung nach London.
- Schreibe, dass du Alice so bald wie möglich besuchen wirst und dass du eine Freundin /einen Freund mitbringen wirst.
- Ihr habt bereits angefangen, Geld für den Flug zu sparen.
- Bedaure, dass sie wegen der Quiz-Show im Fernsehen tyrannisiert wurde.
- Schreibe, dass es vernünftig war, dass sie sofort mit ihren Eltern, den Lehrkräften und der Schulleitung sprach.
- Berichte, dass auch in deiner Klasse ein Mitschüler (Patrick) tyrannisiert wurde, weil er in einem sehr bekannten Fußballverein trainiert. Selbst seine besten Freunde waren sehr eifersüchtig. Sie ärgerten ihn, es wurde immer schlimmer und niemand half ihm.
- Erkläre, dass es an deiner alten Schule Mediatoren und Mediatorinnen gab, mit denen man über seine Probleme sprechen konnte. Sie lösten die Konflikte zwischen dem Fußballstar und seinen Mitschülern /Mitschülerinnen mit Worten, ohne dass jemand verletzt wurde. Patrick wurde danach nicht mehr tyrannisiert.
- Bedaure, dass du Alice nicht helfen konntest.
- Drücke die Hoffnung aus, dass niemand sie in Zukunft mehr tyrannisieren wird.
- Bitte Alice, bald zu antworten und auch ihre Eltern zu grüßen.

Topic 5: Sasha

1 Sasha is only 15, but she is already a star.
She has a fantastic voice and has had several
huge world-wide hits. She travels all over the
world and meets a lot of people but the most
5 important person in her life is her best friend,
Tina.

Sasha: 'Tina and I have known each other for years, long before I ever made a
record. We go to the same school and like the same clothes, jewellery and
make-up. Tina's got quite a cool life. It's more normal than mine. She has an
10 older brother who drives us around. We both like rollerblading and going to the
cinema. I don't think all my fame and money has made any difference to Tina.
We don't talk about my work, as we have better things to talk about, for
example all the gossip at school!

I'm an only child and I'm with my parents all the time because they travel
15 with me. My parents and I argue more, but our relationship has grown stronger.
Tina and I never argue.

I'll keep on singing as long as it lasts. But I don't mind if it doesn't. I've
never really grown used to it all.'

Tina: 'The success hasn't changed Sasha at all. I am much more self-conscious
20 than her, worrying about my hair or what boys think of me. She's always been
quite confident. Boys give her more attention, but none of it has gone to her
head.

At school, she finds it hard too, but the other girls are just jealous. The
schoolwork isn't a problem. When she's away she has two teachers with her,
25 so when she comes back she has learnt more than we have!

When she's 21 and can spend all her money she wants to take me and two
other friends to New York (shopping!), then to the Caribbean. I've already
been on holiday with Sasha and her parents. That's nice, but being friends with
her is the most important.'

Adapted from 'Life Support' by Stephanie Dennison, The Observer Magazine, November 12, 2000, p. 94

Vocabulary

fame (line 11): *Ruhm*
gossip (line 13): *Geschwätz, Gerede*
self-conscious (line 19): *befangen, gehemmt*
confident (line 21): *selbstbewusst, zuversichtlich*
jealous (line 23): *eifersüchtig*

Working on the text

48 Tick (✓) the right answer.

a Sasha and Tina met ...

☐ when Sasha made her first record.

☐ a long time ago.

☐ after Sasha had made lots of records.

☐ a few weeks ago.

b Sasha and Tina both ...

☐ like the same music.

☐ have normal lives.

☐ make records.

☐ like the same make-up.

c Sasha and Tina talk about ...

☐ boys.

☐ what happens when Sasha is travelling.

☐ music.

☐ what happens at school.

d Sasha ...

☐ doesn't think singing is all-important.

☐ thinks that singing is the most important thing in the world.

☐ wants to continue singing all her life.

☐ wants to stop singing.

e Tina says that ...

☐ Sasha thinks about boys all the time.

☐ none of the boys want to speak to Sasha.

☐ more boys want to talk to Sasha than to her.

☐ Sasha isn't worried about her hair.

f Tina says that Sasha ...

☐ doesn't have to go to school.

☐ has two teachers at school.

☐ is jealous of other girls at school.

☐ is good at her schoolwork.

g Tina and Sasha ...

☐ have been to New York together.

☐ have been on holiday together.

☐ have spent all of Sasha's money.

☐ only have two other friends.

49 Match the beginnings and endings of the sentences.

A Sasha and Tina don't talk about Sasha's singing because

B Sasha is an only child because

C Sasha is always with her parents because

D Sasha disagrees with her parents quite often but

(1) she doesn't have arguments with Tina.

(2) they travel around with her.

(3) they have other things to discuss.

(4) she doesn't have any sisters or brothers.

(5) she has got quite a cool life.

A	B	C	D

50 Complete the list: Tick (✓) the correct person(s).

Sasha	Tina	Sasha and Tina	
			… never argue.
			… travels a lot.
			… has a brother.
			… like the same jewellery.
			… earns a lot of money.
			… plan a trip to the Caribbean.

51 Find a sentence with almost the same meaning. Tick (✓) the right answer.

a Sasha: 'I don't think all my fame and money has made any difference to Tina.'

☐ They're best friends because of Sasha's fame and money.

☐ Success hasn't changed Sasha.

☐ Tina is jealous.

b Sasha: 'I've never grown used to it all.'

☐ I've never done it all.

☐ It hasn't become normal for me to be a star.

☐ It helped that I've grown used to be a star.

c Tina: 'She's always been quite confident.'

☐ She's always been worried about her hair.

☐ She's always been optimistic.

☐ She's always been self-conscious.

Language

52 Sasha often travels to the USA. People in Britain and the USA sometimes use different words. Find the missing ones.

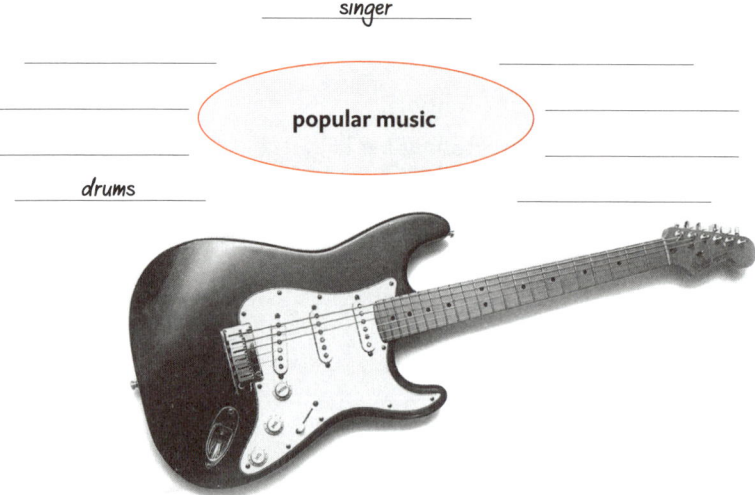

autumn	_fall_
_____	elevator
film	_____
_____	vacation
luggage	_____
lorry	_____
_____	cab
underground	_____
_____	highway
petrol station	_____

53 Popular music – fill the word web.

singer

_____   _____

_____   **popular music**   _____

_____   _____

drums   _____

54 Jobs – what do they do?

A hairdresser ...	... flies a rocket.
A florist ...	... makes websites for the internet.
A car mechanic ...	... builds houses.
A baker ...	... does people's hair.
A website designer ...	... helps sick people.
An astronaut ...	... makes bread and cakes.
An office clerk ...	... works in a flower shop.
A vet ...	... repairs cars.
A nurse ...	... types letters, organises meetings.
A bricklayer ...	... decorates shop windows.
A window dresser ...	... looks after sick animals.

Grammar

Present *perfect simple* – Die 2. Vergangenheit

Das *present perfect simple* beschreibt
- Situationen oder Handlungen, die in der **Vergangenheit begannen und bis zum Sprechzeitpunkt andauern**.
  Beispiel: I have talked to him for hours and hours.

- das Ergebnis einer Tätigkeit oder die Folgen einer Handlung, die zwar vorüber ist, aber **Auswirkungen auf die Gegenwart** hat.
  Beispiel: Tom has broken his leg. He can't go in-line skating.

- wenn etwas **gerade geschehen** ist. Das *present perfect simple* steht dabei häufig mit *just*:
  Beispiel: I've just come home.

Das *present perfect simple* steht oft in Zusammenhang mit folgenden Ausdrücken:
since, for, just, until now, so far, already, ever, never, not yet

- **Beachte:** *Since* (seit) wird verwendet, wenn es sich um einen bestimmten **Zeitpunkt** in der Vergangenheit handelt, an dem das Ereignis begann; *for* **(seit)** wird gebraucht, wenn es sich um einen **Zeitraum** handelt, der bis in die Gegenwart reicht.

They **have been** married <u>since 1991</u>.　　They've <u>lived</u> in San Francisco <u>for 3 years</u>.

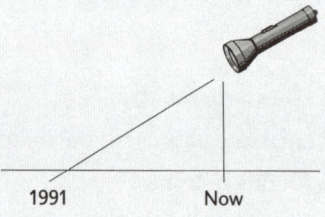
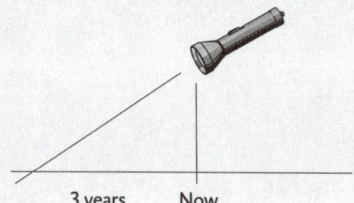

1991	Now	3 years	Now

Wie bildest du das *present perfect* simple?
- Für die **Bildung** des present perfect simple verwendest du **have/has + past participle**.
  Beispiele: I have played football.
  　　　　　Sasha has eaten kangaroo steaks.

- Verneinte Sätze im present perfect simple bildest du mit **haven't/hasn't + past participle**.
  Beispiele: I haven't seen Tom. I've just come in.
  　　　　　Tom hasn't tried Indian food.
  　　　　　He hasn't been to an Indian restaurant so far.

- **Fragen** im present perfect simple bildest du mit **have/has+ Subjekt + past participle**.
  Beispiele: Have you done your homework? – Yes, I have.
  　　　　　Has she ever been to South America? – No she hasn't.

55 Ask and answer these questions.

Tobias is on a school exchange visit in Great Britain and is living with the family of an English student. At breakfast the English student asks him:

a   Have you ever had grapefruit juice before?

(often) – Yes, *I've often drunk / had* _____ it.

b   (eat bacon, eggs and grilled tomatoes)

Have _____ for breakfast? – No, I haven't.

c   (drink English tea)

_____? – No, at home we drink Chinese tea.

d   (try scones with clotted cream)

_____? – No, I _____ scones with clotted cream before. But I would like to try them.

56 Say what has happened.

a   You can see a broken shop window. What has happened?

(thief / break) *A thief has broken the shop window.* _____.

b   You can see a boy crying. What has happened?

(lose / purse)

A boy _____.

c   You can see a postman with a hole in his trousers. What has happened?

(dog / bite)

_____.

d   You can see a pair of trainers on the ground. What has happened?

(drop / trainers)

Somebody _____.

e   You can see a young man lying in the street. What has happened?

(have / accident)

_____.

57 Say it in English using the present perfect. Put the English words in the right order.

a Frage Tina, ob sie jemals in Australien gewesen ist.
Australia / you / ever / have / to / been / Tina

b Sage, dass du noch nie die USA besucht hast.
never / USA / visited / I / the / have

c Frage, ob Sasha je das Fahren mit dem Mountainbike ausprobiert hat.
Sasha / ever / mountain biking / has / tried

d Erkläre, dass du noch nie auf einer Schuldisco gewesen bist.
been / a / have / to / never / school disco / I

e Sage, dass dein Freund seit zwei Wochen nicht angerufen hat.
called / for / my / two / friend / weeks / hasn't

Text Production

Sprachliche Mittel: Nützliche Adjektive – Verhaltensweisen und Gefühle

(1) **beunruhigt, ängstlich**
worried
frightened
scared
troubled

(2) **traurig, niedergeschlagen**
sad
depressed

(3) **schockiert, bestürzt**
shocked
upset

(4) **enttäuscht, frustriert**
disappointed
saddened
frustrated

(5) **verletzt**
hurt
wounded

(6) **verärgert, wütend**
angry
annoyed
furious

(7) **freundlich, nett**
You're very friendly/nice.
That's very kind of you.

(8) **hilfsbereit**
helpful
cooperative

(9) **überrascht, aufgeregt**
surprised
nervous
excited

(10) **Glück haben**
to be lucky

(11) **glücklich, erfreut**
glad
happy
delighted

(12) **ruhig, zufrieden**
quiet
calm
comfortable
relaxed

58 Cartoon

Sieh dir den Cartoon genau an. Beschreibe, was und wen du siehst.
Erkläre dann, worum es in dem Cartoon geht.

Topic 6: Sadiq's journey

1 Sadiq Hanafi's journey to England from Afghanistan took seven months. The
Taliban put his father in prison and the rest of the family escaped to a refugee
camp in Peshawar in the north of Pakistan. Sadiq wanted to go to England but
he had neither papers nor money. In order to pay for Sadiq's journey his
5 mother sold the family land for £6500. 'We either sell the land or spend the
rest of our lives in this camp', his mother said.

Sadiq immediately left on his long journey while his family stayed in Peshawar. He crossed Pakistan and Iran by bus. 'We got through Iran without too
much trouble.' he says. 'But crossing the mountains into Turkey is dangerous.
10 We had to wait for 15 days until the weather got really bad. Then the soldiers
left the mountains. We started climbing as soon as it started snowing. It was
very, very cold and then, after about five hours, the wolves attacked.'

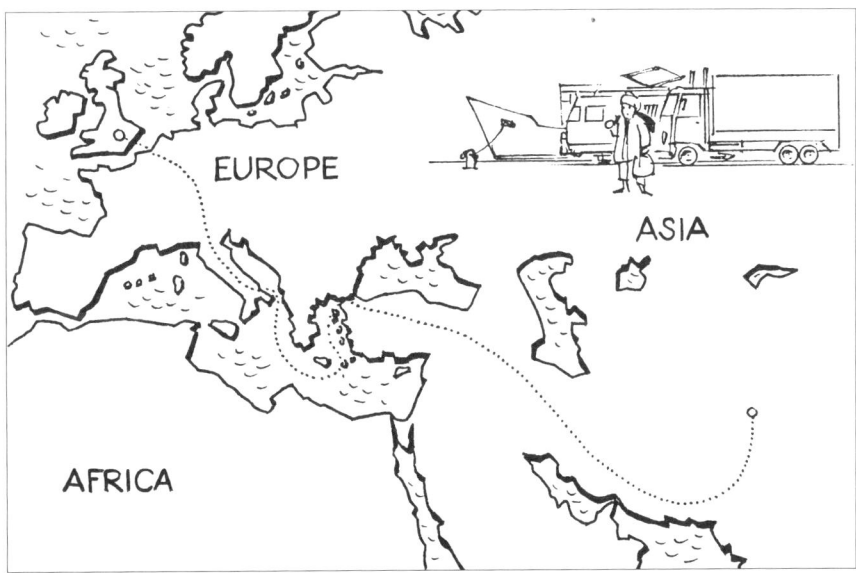

After a 1400 km ride across Turkey in the back of a truck Sadiq spent two
months in Istanbul. He worked in a clothing factory for very little money in
15 order to pay for a boat out of Turkey. Sadiq was lucky – he only spent two
months there. As soon as he had enough money he left on a large fishing boat
for Italy. 'The sea was rough and there were 300 people on board. We had neither food nor drink. The people started praying and crying and I really thought
I was dead. But while everyone was crying a Greek military boat rescued us.'

20 The Greek boat took them to a Greek
island but Sadiq doesn't remember
the name. From there he took another
boat in order to get to Bari in southern
Italy. From there he took a train to
25 Rome where he got inside a truck
going to Britain. 'I got in while no-one
was looking and hid under boxes of
washing powder. It was either that or
be caught by the police.' No-one
30 searched Sadiq's lorry and he reached
London seven months after leaving
Pakistan. As soon as he got to London
he contacted his family.

In Afghanistan, he wanted to be a doctor. Now he is working in an all-night
35 shop in south London in order to send money to his family.

Adapted from 'Sadiq's 7-month journey' by John Crace, Guardian Education, July 3, 2001

Vocabulary

Taliban (line 2): *extreme religiös-politische Gruppierung in Afghanistan*
refugee camp (line 2 f.): *Flüchtlingslager*
neither … nor (line 4): *weder … noch*
in order to (line 4): *um … zu*
either … or (line 5): *entweder … oder*
as soon as (line 11): *sobald*
to rescue (line 19): *retten*
to hide, hid, hidden (*irregular verb*, line 27): *sich verstecken*

Working on the text

59 Tick (✓) the right answer.

a Sadiq's family …

☐ went to England with him.

☐ stayed in Afghanistan.

☐ couldn't give him any money.

☐ spent the rest of their lives in a camp.

b Sadiq travelled through Iran …

☐ on foot.

☐ by truck.

☐ by car.

☐ by bus.

c Sadiq got into Turkey …

☐ without too much trouble.

☐ although it wasn't safe.

☐ quickly.

☐ on his own.

d Sadiq worked in a factory in Istanbul so that he could …

☐ buy clothes.

☐ send money to his family.

☐ pay for a long ride on a truck.

☐ get on a boat and leave Turkey.

e On board there …

☐ were lots of people.

☐ were some dead people.

☐ were Greek soldiers.

☐ was plenty to eat and drink.

f Sadiq travelled from Greece to London by …

☐ bus, train and plane.

☐ boat, train and truck.

☐ boat, bicycle and bus.

☐ car, plane and truck.

g In Rome Sadiq hid in a lorry when …

☐ the driver washed it.

☐ the police searched it.

☐ no-one noticed.

☐ it was dark.

60 Match the beginnings and endings of the sentences:

A Sadiq started climbing the mountains when

B The soldiers left the mountains when

C The wolves attacked when

D Sadiq got in touch with his family when

(1) the weather got very bad.

(2) he reached London.

(3) it started snowing.

(4) it was very, very cold.

(5) he left Istanbul.

A	B	C	D

61 Sadiq's journey: What happened where?
Give examples from the text. Complete the sentences.

a In Pakistan and Iran

He crossed
Pakistan and
Iran by bus.

b In Istanbul he worked
in a _____

c On a large fishing boat he
left for _____

d On a military boat he
travelled to a _____
_____

e In Italy he took
a _____ to _____

f On his way to _____
he hid inside a _____.

g In London he contacted
his _____

62 Find a sentence with almost the same meaning. Tick (✓) the right answer.

a Sadiq's mother: 'We either sell the land or spend the rest of our lives in this camp.'

☐ 'We have to decide to stay here for the rest of our lives or to sell our land.'

☐ 'We sell the land and spend the rest of our lives in this camp.'

☐ 'If we sell the land we will still have to stay in the camp.'

b Sadiq: 'We got through Iran without too much trouble.'

☐ They had problems on their way through Iran.

☐ Crossing Iran was dangerous.

☐ It wasn't difficult for him to travel through Iran.

c Sadiq: '… But while everyone was crying a Greek military boat rescued us.'

☐ The refugees were safe on the Greek military boat.

☐ The people on the large fishing boat were hungry.

☐ He cried when he was rescued by Greek soldiers.

d Sadiq: 'I got in a truck in Italy while no-one was looking. It was either that or be caught by the police.'

☐ He had no choice. He had to hide in the truck or the police would have caught him.

☐ The police caught him when he got in a truck in Italy.

☐ He hid inside a truck but somebody saw him.

e Sadiq: 'Now I work in an all-night shop in south London in order to send money to my family.'

☐ He works every night.

☐ He tries to earn money to help his family far away.

☐ He likes his job in an all-night shop in south London.

Language

63 English sounds – Which word is it? Complete the short newspaper article.

A risky journey

Last night about 300 ['piːpl] _____ on board a fishing

boat were ['reskjuːd] _____ by the Italian navy.

The [ˌrefjʊ'dʒiːs] _____ on board had neither

[fuːd] _____ nor drink. Their ['deɪndʒrəs] _____

trip ended safely after they had arrived at the military boat.

64 On Sadiq's journey he used a lot of vehicles – you know some more.
Fill in the word web about "transport".

_____ bus _____

_____

_____ (**transport**) _____

_____ helicopter _____

_____

_____

65 Match each container with its contents.

basket	flowers
vase	coins
safe	exercise books
purse	shopping
bin	washing powder
box	jewellery, secret documents
school bag	clothes
suitcase	letter
envelope	waste paper

Grammar

Conjunctions – Bindewörter

Bindewörter **verbinden zwei gleichartige Sätze oder Haupt- und Nebensätze**.
Wie im Deutschen kannst du auch im Englischen Sätze mit Bindewörtern verbinden,
zum Beispiel:

although	obwohl, obgleich	first	zuerst
after that	danach	in order to	um … zu, damit
as	als (zeitlich)	neither … nor	weder … noch
as soon as	sobald	so that	sodass
because	weil	then	dann, danach
but	aber	when	als, wenn (zeitlich)
either … or	entweder … oder	while	während

Die folgenden **Beispielsätze** zeigen dir, wie du die Bindewörter anwenden kannst:

- **but** oder **although**
  Beispiele: Although he was in a hurry he listened to me patiently.
  Obwohl er in Eile war, hörte er mir geduldig zu.
  He smiled, but he didn't say a word.
  Er lächelte, aber er sagte kein (einziges) Wort.

- **first … then, when, while, as soon as – relationship in time**
  Beispiele: First you knock on the door, then you come into my room.
  Erst klopfst du an die Tür, danach kommst du in mein Zimmer.
  I'll go when I'm ready.
  Ich werde gehen, wenn/sobald ich fertig bin.
  My mother bought a tablet for me while I was in hospital.
  Meine Mutter kaufte ein Tablet für mich, während ich im Krankenhaus war.
  You can meet your friends as soon as you finish your homework.
  Du kannst deine Freunde treffen, sobald du deine Hausaufgabe beendet hast.

- **in order to, so that**
  Beispiele: He worked hard in order to pass his exams.
  Er arbeitete (lernte) viel, um seine Prüfungen zu bestehen.
  The wind was too strong so that they couldn't go surfing.
  Der Wind war zu stark, sodass sie nicht surfen gehen konnten.

- **because**
  Beispiel: She went shopping because there was no food in the fridge.
  Sie ging einkaufen, weil nichts zu essen im Kühlschrank war.

- **either … or** oder **neither … nor**
  Beispiele: We can either have dinner at home or we can go to a restaurant.
  Wir können entweder zu Hause Abend essen oder in ein Restaurant gehen.
  I can eat neither garlic nor onions. I'm allergic to them.
  Ich kann weder Knoblauch noch Zwiebeln essen. Ich bin allergisch dagegen.

66 Choose the right conjunction.

a As soon as / During / While   the Taliban put his father in prison his family escaped to a refugee camp in Pakistan.

b First / After that / When   Sadiq started his dangerous journey.

c He worked in Istanbul   up to / in order to / as to / for to   earn some money for the boat trip to Italy.

d While / As soon as / Before   he had enough money he left on a large fishing boat for Italy.

e In Rome he got inside a truck to Britain   then / afterwards / while   no-one was looking.

f Finally, he arrived in London safely   also / although / or   it was a very long and dangerous journey.

67 Say it in English. Think of using the correct conjunction.

a Sage, dass du hart arbeitest, um die Abschlussprüfungen zu bestehen.

b Sage, dass du deine Freunde treffen wirst, wenn du Zeit hast.

c Sage, dass du oft ins Kino gehst, obwohl du wenig Taschengeld bekommst.

d Sage, dass du Skilaufen gehst, sobald es in den Bergen schneit.

e Sage, dass du erst ein Geschenk kaufst und danach auf die Geburtstagsfeier gehen wirst.

Text Production

68 Say it in English.
Was sagst du, wenn …

a … du dich am Telefon meldest?

_____

_____

b … du Mitgefühl äußern willst mit allen Menschen, die in Flüchtlingslagern
leben?

_____

_____

c … du der Meinung bist, dass alle Menschen auf der Welt frei und gleich
(equal) sein sollten?

_____

_____

d … du die Hoffnung äußerst, dass du deine Familie bald wieder sehen wirst?

_____

_____

e … du dir einen Rat holen willst, welchen neuen Job du wählen solltest?

_____

_____

f … du keine Angst vor einem Vorstellungsgespräch hast?

_____

_____

g … dir keine Sorgen über deine Zukunft machst?

_____

_____

Sprachliche Mittel: **Was schreibst du in einem sachlichen Brief/ einer sachlichen E-Mail?**

(1) **Anrede**
Dear Mr …,
Dear Ms …,
Dear Mrs …,
Dear Sir,
Dear Madam,
Dear Sir or Madam,

(2) **Beginn: Anlass**
I am writing to …

(3) **Anfrage**
Could you (send me, tell me where / when …) …?
Can you …, please?
I hope that you may be able to …

(4) eigene **Zukunftspläne vorstellen**
I will … next summer.
In July I'll …

(5) eigene **Fähigkeiten darlegen**
I am good at …
I am not bad at …

(6) eigene **Vorlieben ausdrücken**
I am interested in …
I like … (best).
My favourite … is …

(7) **Anlagen im Text erwähnen**
I enclose my …
You will find my … enclosed.

(8) **Dank ausdrücken**
I would like to thank you for helping me.
I would like to thank you for your help.

(9) **Hoffnung ausdrücken**
I look forward to hearing from you soon.
I hope you will consider my application.

(10) **Grußformel am Ende**
Yours sincerely, (wird verwendet, wenn der Name des Adressaten genannt wird)
Yours faithfully, (wird verwendet, wenn der Name des Adressaten unbekannt ist)
Yours,

69 Verfasse ein Bewerbungsschreiben
Im Lake District National Park in Großbritannien wird ein *summer camp* für Jugendliche aus aller Welt stattfinden. Dort werden neben Ausflügen und Besichtigungen auch Ferienjobs angeboten: in den Büros oder in der Küche der Jugendherberge, in der Gärtnerei oder bei der Kinderbetreuung. Die Jugendlichen arbeiten an Wochentagen vier Stunden täglich und bekommen dafür freie Unterkunft und Verpflegung.

Bewirb dich um einen Ferienjob. Dein sachliches Anschreiben sollte mindestens zehn Sätze umfassen. Achte auf die richtige Form (Anschrift, Anrede, Grußformel).

- Stelle dich vor, nenne dein Alter und sage, wo du die Schule besuchst.
- Schreibe, wann du die Schule beenden wirst, und ergänze, was du nach der Schule tun wirst.
- Erwähne, dass du in der Schule von deiner Lehrkraft von dem Sommerferienlager im Lake District erfahren hast.
- Bestimme genau, von wann bis wann du in Großbritannien arbeiten möchtest.
- Erkläre, welche Tätigkeit du während deines Aufenthalts ausüben willst und dass du sehr interessiert an der Arbeit bist.
- Berichte, welche Ferienjobs / Praktika du in Deutschland schon gemacht hast, und erkläre, warum du für diese Arbeit in Großbritannien geeignet bist.
- Schreibe, welche Sprachen du beherrschst.
- Erwähne, dass du deinen Lebenslauf beilegst.
- Drücke die Hoffnung aus, dass deine Bewerbung erfolgreich sein wird und du von der Agentur bald Nachricht bekommen wirst.

Topic 7: Alicia's World Tour Diary

'Hi, Alicia here. Want to know what I get up to on tour?
Well, here's a look at my diary for the day of my first UK concert.'

1 **11 a.m.**
I'm finally in London. Flew in yesterday and still
feel slightly jet-lagged, but of course really excited
to be here at last. I can't tell you how nervous I am,
5 but this is my first world tour! How cool – Frank,
my masseur has just come in and he's going to give
me a massage.
I think having a massage is just one of my all-time
favourite things.

10 **12.30 p.m.**
Just had chicken salad for lunch at my hotel. I can't wait to go shopping – the
shops in London are really hot. But I want to focus on my concert tonight, so
I'm going to go shopping tomorrow.

2.30 p.m.
15 The sound-check – that's when we make sure that the microphones and everything are working – isn't until 4 p.m. but I'm going to leave now. I want to
get there early and then have some sleep. Sleep is one thing I never get enough
of!

5.30 p.m.
20 Sound-check went well and I had some sleep. I'm just going to do an interview
for radio now.

6.30 p.m.
Had a really light meal. Just a small tuna salad. I love tuna so much because it's
not too heavy and I'm going to be dancing a lot tonight. From now on it's time
25 for me to be on my own and think about the show. I can't stop biting my nails!

7.15 p.m.
Time to start warming up. Singing a few of my songs to warm my voice up. I
always drink so much water – it's good for me and my voice. Now it's time to
get changed. I'm going to wear the pink top tonight to start with, instead of
30 the orange one.

8.45 p.m.

Walk with Rob, my security guy, to the side of the stage. My dancers and I all hold hands in a circle to get ourselves ready.

8.55 p. m.

35 Aaarrgh! Show time! I hope it's going to be all right.

Adapted from 'Dear Diary', Top of the Pops Magazine, Issue 69, Nov 2000, pp. 38/39

Vocabulary

slightly (line 3): *leicht*
to focus on (line 12): *sich konzentrieren auf*
tuna (line 23): *Thunfisch*
security (line 32) *Sicherheit*
stage (line 32): *Bühne*

Working on the text

70 Tick (✓) the right answer.

a On arrival Alicia feels . . .

☐ a bit tired.
☐ bored.
☐ calm.
☐ hot.

b Frank has just given Alicia . . .

☐ a message.
☐ a present.
☐ a massage.
☐ a tour guide.

c Alicia isn't going shopping today because . . .

☐ of the weather.
☐ she couldn't wait.
☐ of her lunch.
☐ of the concert.

d At the sound-check Alicia …

☐ does an interview.

☐ makes sure everything is OK.

☐ has some sleep.

☐ has something to eat.

e After her tuna salad Alicia …

☐ sees lots of friends.

☐ has a massage.

☐ gets ready for her show.

☐ still feels hungry.

f Alicia prepares for her concert by …

☐ drinking orange juice.

☐ changing her songs.

☐ washing herself.

☐ singing some songs.

g Before the show starts Alicia …

☐ stands in a circle with her dancers.

☐ sings to her security guy.

☐ holds hands with Rob.

☐ goes for a long walk.

71 Match the beginnings and endings of the sentences.

A Alicia has some sleep

B Alicia has lunch

C Alicia drinks a lot of water

D Alicia hopes everything will be OK

(1) after her massage.

(2) when the show starts.

(3) after the sound-check.

(4) when she warms up.

(5) after her show.

A	B	C	D

72 Cross out the wrong words. Write down the correct ones.

a Alicia is ~~Australian~~.

    American
_____

b Alicia arrived in Great Britain two days ago.

_____

c She thinks the meals in London are really hot.

_____

d The sound-check takes place after the concert.

_____

e She dislikes having a massage.

_____

f With Rob, her fitness trainer, she walks to the side of the stage.

_____

g Alicia is nervous, it's her second world tour.

_____

h She always drinks so much cola.

_____

i She starts warming up by singing a few songs to cool down her voice.

_____

73 Put the sentences into the right order: What happened first?

	She walked to the stage with Rob, her security guy.
	She had some sleep.
	She did an interview for radio.
	She warmed her voice up by singing some of her songs.
	Alicia and her dancers held hands to get themselves ready.
	She went to the sound-check.
	She had a massage.
	She ate a small tuna salad.

Language

74 What do excited fans do?
Match the correct verbs from the list below, use each word only once.

> find out – go to – listen to – love – read – send – visit – watch – wear

Fans

_____	TV interviews and video clips.
_____	Alicia's homepage.
_____	magazines and newspaper articles about Alicia.
_____	Alicia's music best.
_____	her radio interviews.
_____	e-mails to her.
_____	a T-shirt with her photo every day
_____	her concerts.
_____	everything about Alicia

75 Find the other word or expression with the same meaning:

voice	☐
favourite	☐
excited	☐
stage	☐
make sure	☐
circle	☐
diary	☐

1 a round geometric figure
2 to do what is necessary for something to happen
3 where singers or actors perform
4 a book where you write what happens every day
5 very happy because something good is going to happen
6 to be sad, unhappy
7 what you like best
8 a stable
9 the sounds that you make when you speak

76 Alicia likes to go shopping – There are a lot of different shops in London: What do you buy where? Match the items on the left with the shops where you buy them on the right:

newspapers, magazines	pet shop
hamsters, guinea pigs	greengrocer's
meat	tobacconist's
bread, rolls, cakes	newsagent's
cigarettes, cigars	baker's
tea, biscuits, butter	butcher's
fruit, vegetables	antique shop
very old furniture	grocer's
dictionaries	florist's
flowers	bookshop

77 Alicia is American. People in Britain and the USA sometimes use different words. Complete with these words: *pullover – eraser – rucksack – shop – single – stand in line – cookie – bill – post – toilet.*

biscuit   cookie

_____   check

queue   _____

_____   mail

_____   restroom

one-way ticket   _____ ticket

_____   backpack

_____   store

_____   sweater

rubber   _____

Grammar

Adjectives and adverbs – Adjektive und Adverbien

Adjektive beschreiben, wie jemand oder etwas ist. Sie beschreiben **Eigenschaften von Nomen oder Pronomen** und werden deshalb auch **Eigenschaftswörter** genannt.

Beispiel: Alicia is <u>nervous</u> before the concert.

Adverbien (Umstandswörter) bestimmen andere Wörter im Satz ihrem Umstand nach näher: Adjektive, Verben, andere Adverbien, Mengenbezeichnungen und ganze Sätze.

Beispiele: Alicia is <u>extremely</u> <u>nervous</u> before the concert.   → <u>Adjektiv</u> näher bestimmt
Sie ist äußerst nervös vor dem Konzert.

Alicia <u>sings</u> <u>wonderfully</u>.   → <u>Verb</u>
Alicia singt wunderbar.

Her band played <u>very</u> <u>well</u>.   → <u>Adverb</u>
Ihre Band spielte sehr gut.

There were <u>quite</u> <u>a lot of</u> people at the concert.   → <u>Mengenbezeichnung</u>
Es waren ziemlich viele Menschen in dem Konzert.

<u>Fortunately</u>, <u>she managed everything</u>.   → <u>ganzer Satz</u>
Glücklicherweise hat sie alles gemeistert.

Es gibt u. a. Adverbien des Ortes (z. B. *here, there*), der Zeit (z. B. *soon, already*), der Häufigkeit (z. B. *always, often*) und der Art und Weise (z. B. *carefully, beautifully*).

Wie bildest du die Adverbien?

- Die meisten Adverbien werden durch **Anhängen der Endung -ly** gebildet:
  Beispiele: careful – careful<u>ly</u>
  clear – clear<u>ly</u>
  nervous – nervous<u>ly</u>
  quick – quick<u>ly</u>

- **Besonderheiten** bei der Bildung der Adverbien:
  (1) Endet das Adjektiv mit -y, wird das Adverb mit -ily gebildet:
  Beispiele: angry – angri<u>ly</u>
  happy – happi<u>ly</u>
  heavy – heavi<u>ly</u>

  (2) Endet das Adjektiv mit -le, wird dies durch -ly ersetzt.
  Beispiele: gentle – gent<u>ly</u>
  probable – probab<u>ly</u>
  simple – simp<u>ly</u>

  (3) Einige Adverbien haben dieselbe Form wie die entsprechenden Adjektive:
  Beispiele: daily, early, fair, fast, free, hard, wrong

  (4) **Beachte:** Das Adverb von *good* heißt *well*.

78 Mariah's friends are busy tonight. Fill in the gaps with the right form of the adverb.

a Diana is cooking for her friends

_____ (eager).

b Tony is watching the football match

_____ (lazy).

c Ian is looking forward to the musical

_____ (excited).

d Mary is celebrating her birthday

_____ (happy).

79 Find the right adverb to describe how to do things.

write an exam	seriously
live with your family	nervously
do your work	happily
pet your cat	quickly
cross the street	gently
a dog barking	carefully
ride your bike	well
sleep	loudly

80 Meeting a friend. Use adverbs to complete the story.

It was a lovely day in September. The sun was shining _____ (bright), a light breeze was blowing _____ (gentle) and the birds were singing _____ (beautiful), but Mariah didn't notice. She was worried because her work was going _____ (bad) and her boss was terrible. As she was walking _____ (slow) down the road she met her friend Brian. He was on his way to his pub. They talked _____ (serious) about her problems. In the end Brian asked her to work at his pub. Mariah accepted his offer _____ (happy). What a lovely day for her.

Text Production

Sprachliche Mittel: Was sagst du am Telefon?

(1) Wenn du dich **am Telefon melden** willst:
This is … speaking. Can I help you?

(2) Wenn du **jemanden am Telefon verlangen** willst:
Can I speak to …?
Could I speak to …?
Hello, is Mary there?

(3) Wenn du **um Vermittlung bitten** willst:
Could you put me through? …

(4) Wenn du **bedauern** willst, **dass der Angerufene nicht zu sprechen** ist:
Sorry, she's not here at the moment.
Sorry, he's out …

(5) Wenn du dem Anrufer mitteilen willst, dass du **jemanden ans Telefon holen** wirst:
Hold on, I'll get her for you …
Wait a minute, I'll put you through.

(6) Wenn du einen späteren **Rückruf ankündigen / um einen Rückruf bitten** willst:
I'll call back later.
Give me a ring sometime/on Wednesday.

(7) Wenn du **fragen** willst, **ob das Gesagte zu hören war:**
Can you hear me?

(8) Wenn du darum bitten willst, dass dein Gesprächspartner das Gesagte **wiederholt:**
Could you please repeat …?

(9) Wenn du darum bitten willst, dass dir etwas **buchstabiert** wird:
Could you please spell …?

(10) Wenn du dich **für einen Anruf bedanken** willst:
Thanks for phoning …

(11) Wenn du **fragen** willst, **ob jemandem etwas ausgerichtet werden kann:**
Will you give him/her a message?
Can you take a message?

81 Say it in English.

Was sagt du, wenn ...

a ... du am Telefon jemanden verlangst?

_____

b ... du von der Telefonzentrale der Arbeitsstelle deiner Freundin mit ihr verbunden werden willst?

_____

c ... du später noch einmal anrufen wirst?

_____

d ... du fragst, ob der Telefonpartner jemandem etwas ausrichten könnte.

_____

e ... du um Rückruf bittest?

_____

f ... du der Anruferin mitteilst, dass du sie mit deiner Mutter verbinden wirst?

_____

g ... du der Anruferin mitteilst, dass deine Mutter im Moment nicht zu Hause ist?

_____

h ... du die Anruferin bittest, später noch mal anzurufen?

_____

i ... du dich für einen Anruf bedankst?

_____

j ... du darum bittest, dass man dir die Internetadresse buchstabiert?

_____

k ... du etwas nicht verstanden hast und darum bittest, dass das Gesagte noch einmal wiederholt wird?

_____

82 Picture Story: Sarah's Story

Beachte: Deine Bildergeschichte sollte mindestens 10 Sätze umfassen. Achte auf die richtige Zeit.

Fan-Tagebuch – schreiben

vor zwei Wochen – Poster sehen – Popkonzert

Eintrittskarte kaufen

T-Shirt kaufen – sich freuen

Tagebuch schreiben – aufgeregt sein

nachmittags – vorbereiten – schminken

U-Bahn fahren – verwundert sein – wenige Menschen am Bahnsteig

falsches Datum – überrascht sein – morgen

Topic 8: Valentine's Day Visit

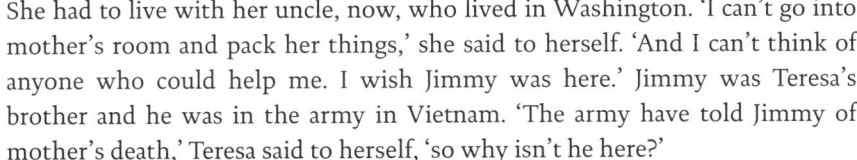

1 It was Valentine's Day, February 14th, 1964. In a small apartment in Baltimore in the USA a woman was alone and there was the sound of crying. It was 18-year-old Teresa who was crying her heart out. But she wasn't sad
5 because of a Valentine card which hadn't come. Teresa was crying because her mother had died two weeks before. Now Teresa had to move out of the apartment. She had to live with her uncle, now, who lived in Washington. 'I can't go into mother's room and pack her things,' she said to herself. 'And I can't think of
10 anyone who could help me. I wish Jimmy was here.' Jimmy was Teresa's brother and he was in the army in Vietnam. 'The army have told Jimmy of mother's death,' Teresa said to herself, 'so why isn't he here?'

Teresa wiped away her tears. But when she opened her eyes she had a great surprise. There was someone else in the apartment. It was Jimmy, her brother,
15 who was standing in front of her. He had his army uniform on and he smiled kindly at her. It was like a dream that had come true.

'Let me help you,' Jimmy said. The brother and sister worked together and packed all the things that were in their mother's room. Teresa was still sad because of her mother's death, but very happy that her brother was with her.
20 'Now,' Jimmy said. 'Let's call a mover.'

'But I've tried,' Teresa said. 'I can't find anyone who can take me.'

'Try again,' Jimmy said.

This time Teresa found a mover that could take her and her things to Washington that same day. While they were waiting for the mover to come the
25 brother and sister sat and held hands, without saying anything.

When the mover arrived Jimmy helped put the things which they had packed in the truck. Then Jimmy took Teresa by the shoulders and said, 'You go with the truck and don't look back. Do what Mother always wanted you to do, and remember, I'll always be with you.'
30 As the truck left Teresa wondered why her brother wasn't going to Washington with her. 'I guess he had to get back to Vietnam,' she said.

On 10th March 1964 Teresa received a telegram which had been sent on from her old address. It was from the army. Her brother Jimmy was dead. He had died in Vietnam on February 14th – the same day on which he was 'with'
35 her in Baltimore.

From The World's Most Spine-Tingling True Ghost Stories © 1993 by Sheila Anne Barry.
Used with permission from Sterling Publishing Co., Inc.

Vocabulary

Valentine's Day (headline): *Festtag für Verliebte; gute Freunde schreiben sich eine liebevoll gestaltete Valentinskarte*
to wipe (line 13): *(weg)wischen*
kindly (line 16): *nett, liebenswürdig*
mover (line 20): *Umzugsunternehmen*
to receive (line 32): *crhalten*

Working on the text

83 Tick (✓) the right answer.

 a Teresa was sad because …

  ☐ she was alone.
  ☐ she hadn't got a Valentine card.
  ☐ it was Valentine's Day.
  ☐ her mother had died.

 b Teresa had to stay …

  ☐ with her uncle now.
  ☐ in Baltimore.
  ☐ in her mother's room.
  ☐ with her brother in Washington.

 c Teresa wanted …

  ☐ the war in Vietnam to end.
  ☐ her brother to leave the army.
  ☐ her brother to help her.
  ☐ her uncle to help her move.

 d Jimmy and Teresa packed …

  ☐ Teresa's things.
  ☐ their mother's things.
  ☐ the mover's things.
  ☐ their uncle's things.

e While they were waiting for the truck the brother and sister . . .

☐ didn't talk to each other.

☐ talked a lot.

☐ talked about the war in Vietnam.

☐ talked about their mother.

f Teresa's telegram said that Jimmy . . .

☐ had to go back to Vietnam.

☐ wasn't going to Washington with her.

☐ died on Valentine's day.

☐ was with her in Washington.

84 True, false or not in the text?

		true	false	not in the text
a	Teresa was a 20-year-old girl living in Baltimore.	☐	☐	☐
b	Teresa was crying because she didn't get a Valentine card.	☐	☐	☐
c	Her mother was buried in Baltimore.	☐	☐	☐
d	Teresa had to move out of the apartment.	☐	☐	☐
e	She had to live alone in Washington now.	☐	☐	☐
f	Teresa's brother was serving with the army in Vietnam.	☐	☐	☐
g	Her brother called a mover who could take her and her things to Washington.	☐	☐	☐
h	Her brother helped put everything in the mover's truck.	☐	☐	☐
i	As the truck left Teresa's brother decided to go to Washington with her.	☐	☐	☐
j	Teresa's brother had died on his way to Baltimore on February 14th.	☐	☐	☐
k	Jimmy was buried in Baltimore like his mother.	☐	☐	☐

85 People often believe in ghost stories – do you? Give two reasons.

_____

_____

_____

_____

_____

Language

86 Find the opposite – Teresa's situation.

a Teresa's bed was very <u>old</u>, so she decided to buy a _____*new*_____ one.

b Teresa was _____ because her mother had died, but she felt <u>happy</u> to have her brother near her.

c She sometimes goes to the cinema. She prefers _____ movies to <u>boring</u> ones.

d She really _____ her brother Jimmy, though she <u>hated</u> his decision to serve with the army.

e That morning she was a bit <u>lazy</u>, but when she thought of her brother she started to be very _____.

f The movers were carrying _____ things while she was carrying the <u>light</u> ones like her clothes.

g On the motorway they drove _____, but in town they could only drive <u>slowly</u>.

h At the end of the story she was the only one of her family to be <u>alive</u> as her mother and brother were _____.

87   Where is it? – Name the places.

The place where young flowers
and plants are cultivated.

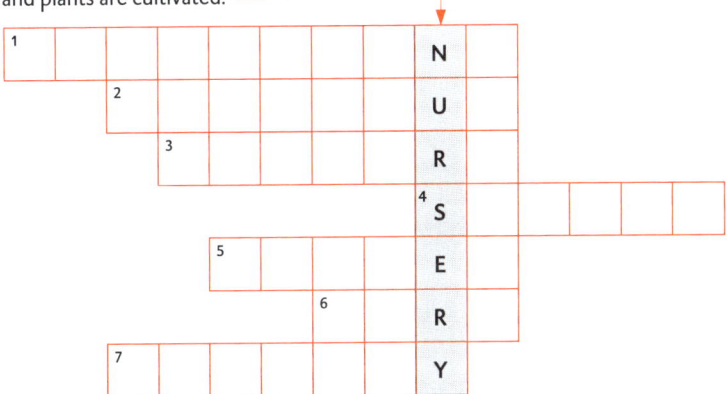

(1) The place where you sit, eat and drink out.

(2) The place where small fish are kept.

(3) The place where plays and musicals are performed.

(4) The place where pupils study.

(5) The place, often in the open, where many different sorts of goods can be bought.

(6) The place where you find cows, sheep, pigs, chicken etc.

(7) The room where doctors receive their patients.

88   Find the right word: see, watch or look?

a   There's a cat in the tree over there. Can you _____ it?

b   I'm afraid not. I cannot _____ very well. I need glasses.

c   Oh, please be careful! _____ out for cars when you cross the street.

d   Philip, please switch on the light. I can't _____ what I'm reading any longer.

e   Haven't you got eyes in your head, little boy? Why don't you _____ where you're going?

f   On the phone: Peter, can you come and _____ me next Saturday?

g   We could have dinner and _____ TV afterwards.

h   Do you like to _____ sports on TV?

Grammatik

> **Simple present – einfaches Präsens**
>
> Das *simple present* verwendet man, um regelmäßig wiederkehrende Aktionen zu beschreiben. Mit dem *simple present* beschreibst du also, was du **immer wieder machst** (oder auch nicht), bzw. **was öfter geschieht**.
>
> **Wie bildest du das *simple present*?**
>
> • Das *simple present* bildest du mit der **Grundform des Verbs**.
>
> | I | often/usually/never/ | **watch** | TV. |
> | He/She/It | sometimes … | **watches** | |
> | We/You/They | | **watch** | |
>
> • Die **Verneinung** bildest du mit *don't* oder *doesn't* und der Grundform des Verbs.
>
> | I | **don't** | | |
> | He/She/It | **doesn't** | skate | without a helmet. |
> | We/You/They | **don't** | | |
>
> • Die **Frage** bildest du mit *do* oder *does* und der Grundform des Verbs.
>
> | **Do** | I | have to wash | the dishes? |
> | **Does** | he/she/it | go | for a walk? |
> | **Do** | we/you/they | meet | at 8 o'clock? |

89 Put in the present tense forms of the verbs in brackets.

Tina's uncle, who is thirty-five years older than she is, _____ (love) Elvis Presley's music. He _____ (buy) a lot of singles and CDs. He _____ (say): "I think Elvis Presley's music _____ (be) great." But Tina usually _____ (not like) Rock'n'Roll. She _____ (prefer) modern pop music. She often _____ (go) to concerts of her favourite band.

90 An Interview with Teresa. Can you find the questions?

Example: What's your name?   Teresa.

a _____   I'm eighteen.

b _____   In Washington.

c _____   No, I live with my uncle.

d _____   I listen to pop music, read books and watch TV.

e _____   Yes, his name is Jimmy.

Present progressive – die Verlaufsform des Präsens

Das *present progressive* verwendest du, um auszudrücken, dass **etwas gerade geschieht**.

Wie bildest du das *present progressive*?

- Das *present progressive* bildest du mit einer Form von **to be** und der **Grundform des Verbs**, an die die **Endung -ing** hinzugefügt wird.

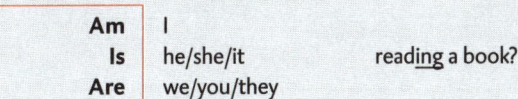

I	**am**	
He/She/It	**is**	reading a book.
We/You/They	**are**	

- Die **Verneinung** des *present progressive* bildest du, indem du **not** einfügst. Die Verneinung wird meistens abgekürzt ("I'm not reading").

I	**am not / I'm not**	
He/She/It	**is not / isn't**	reading a book.
We/You/They	**are not / aren't**	

- In **Fragesätzen** wird die **Form von to be** an den **Anfang des Satzes** gestellt.

Am	I	
Is	he/she/it	reading a book?
Are	we/you/they	

91 What are the people doing?

wait for the bus	take a photo	eat a sandwich
look at a map	drink a cup of coffee	use a mobile phone
read a newspaper		

A *is reading a newspaper.* _____

B _____

C _____

D _____

E _____

F _____

G _____

92 What is Teresa doing on February 14th?

a Teresa is _____ alone in her apartment.

b She is _____ for a Valentine card.

c Teresa _____ _____ because her mother died two weeks ago.

d Teresa _____ _____ her tears from her eyes.

e She _____ _____ her mother's clothes and possessions.

Text Production

> **Sprachliche Mittel: Wie gehst du auf deinen Gesprächspartner ein?**
>
> (1) Wenn du dich **nach dem Befinden erkundigen** willst:
> How are you?
> How are things going?
>
> (2) Wenn du **Besorgnis ausdrücken** willst:
> What was wrong with you?
> What's the matter? You look worried.
> Are you worried about …?
> Are you afraid of …?
>
> (3) Wenn du eine **Meinung erfragen** willst:
> What do you think of …?
> What's your opinion?
> Are you happy about that?
>
> (4) Wenn du deine **Zustimmung kundtun** willst:
> A good idea.   I'm sure your're right.
> Brilliant!   That's correct.
> Terrific!   I agree.
>
> (5) Wenn du **Ablehnung äußern** willst:
> I don't agree.
> I think that's wrong.
> I'd never …
>
> (6) Wenn du **um Rat fragen** willst:
> What would you do?
> What do you think I should do?
>
> (7) Wenn du einen **Rat geben** willst:
> I think you should …
> You should better …

(8) Wenn du **Wünsche, Pläne erfragen** willst:
What are you going to do?
Have you got any plans?

(9) Wenn du die **Bedeutung / Dringlichkeit erfragen** willst:
Is it important?
How important is it (to you)?
Is it urgent?

(10) Wenn du ein **Versprechen geben** willst:
I promise …

(11) Wenn du **über notwendige Tätigkeiten (Pflichten) sprechen** willst:
I have to …
We must …

93 Say it in English.
Deinem Freund geht es nicht gut. Er ist auf der Suche nach einem neuen Job.
Was sagt du, wenn …

a … du fragen willst, wie es ihm geht?

_____

b … wenn du wissen willst, ob er sich Sorgen um seinen Job macht?

_____

c … wenn du wissen willst, was er von Teilzeitjobs *(part-time jobs)* hält?

_____

d … du deinem Freund den Rat gibst, mit seinen Eltern zu sprechen?

_____

e … du wissen willst, ob er irgendwelche Pläne hat?

_____

f … wissen willst, wie wichtig ein gut bezahlter *(well-paid)* Job für ihn ist?

_____

g … versprichst, ihm bei der Jobsuche zu helfen?

_____

94 Picture Story

Beachte: Deine Bildergeschichte sollte mindestens 10 Sätze umfassen.

Denke daran, Sandras Gefühle/Ängste zu beschreiben.

Black Magic?

Sandras neuer Freund – glücklich

einladen – Abendessen

Tisch decken – zwei Fische

klingeln – Türe öffnen – Blumenstrauß

unglaublich – ein Teller leer

entsetzt – schwarze Magie?

umarmen – nicht an Geister glauben

Katze ‚Blacky' – Fisch gestohlen

Topic 9: Body Piercing

1 What is **body piercing**? It's the latest fashion for
teenagers – holes in your nose, or ear or even tongue.
You can put silver rings in the holes or even diamonds! It's not only the latest fashion, but it is also
5 the latest cause of arguments between teenagers and
their parents.

Sarah Lemmon is 14 and lives in Cambridge. Sarah
wants a hole in her tongue but her mother, Tracy, 38,
says no. 'If you want to pierce your tongue you'll
10 have to wait until you're older,' Tracy says.

Sarah, who goes to Impington Village College, says
she will win the argument: 'It doesn't matter what age you are. Do it if it will
make you happy. It's my body so I'll do what I want with it. If mum keeps on
saying no, I'll do it anyway. Mum knows that.'

15 Ali Wiseman owns *Characters*, a Cambridge shop specialising in piercing.
He has strict rules. 'There is no law about body piercing – you can do it at any
age. But I'll only do piercing on someone under 18 if their parents are with
them. But it worries me because other shops are not so strict. And if I don't do
it the teenagers will try and pierce themselves. That can be terribly dangerous.
20 If you make a mistake, you'll get terribly bad blood poisoning. So it's better to
go to a shop. And if we don't do it for them, someone else will.'

Characters also does **'temptoos'** – these are coloured pictures on the skin
but unlike tattoos are not permanent. If you have a temptoo it will last a maxi-
mum of seven years.

25 Is it expensive? If you have a temptoo it will cost about £45 and will take up
to three hours. You can have a temptoo at any age but if you want a real **tattoo**
you'll have to wait until you're 18. If you want a hole in your tongue it will
cost you £35.

You can also have **'smile gems'**. These look like diamonds and are stuck to
30 the teeth so they shine when they smile. If you want a smile gem it will cost
£20 and will last for up to three years.

Roger Cooey of Cambridge City Council says the law is out of date. 'If we don't control body piercing better there will be problems. The law needs to catch up with what is happening.'

35   'If parents want to come in and talk about their worries,' Ali says, 'we'll give them good advice. In fact, a lot of parents actually end up having piercing themselves!'

Adapted from 'Parents Facing Piercing Questions from teenagers' by Katy Edwards, Cambridge Evening News, March 1, 2001, pp. 24/25

Vocabulary

cause of arguments (line 5): *Grund, Anlass für Streitigkeiten*
keep on saying no (line 13 f.): *weiterhin Nein sagen*
to worry (line 18): *sich Sorgen machen*
poisoning (line 20): *Vergiftung*
to stick, stuck, stuck (irregular verb, line 29): *festkleben*
to catch up with, caught, caught (*irregular verb*, line 34): *hier: sich anpassen an*
advice (line 36): *Rat*

Working on the text

95   Tick (✓) the right answer.

  a   Sarah wants ...

    ☐ a hole in her tongue.

    ☐ a hole in her nose.

    ☐ an argument with her mother.

    ☐ a silver ring.

  b   Tracy says that Sarah can ...

    ☐ never have a piercing.

    ☐ have a piercing when she's 38.

    ☐ have a piercing now.

    ☐ have a piercing in a few years' time

  c   Sarah says that she ...

    ☐ will have the piercing at school.

    ☐ won't do what her mother tells her.

    ☐ won't win the argument.

    ☐ knows that her mother will win the argument.

d In Britain you can do body piercing ...

☐ when you're over 18.

☐ when you're with your parents.

☐ whatever age you are.

☐ only when you're in a shop.

e The shop owner, Ali, says that ...

☐ all the body piercing shops are the same.

☐ he helps teenagers to pierce themselves.

☐ body piercing can be very dangerous.

☐ it's better for parents to do the body piercing.

f 'Temptoos' can last for ...

☐ no more than seven years.

☐ three hours.

☐ 18 years.

☐ ever.

g Roger Cooey says that the law on body piercing ...

☐ should be up to date.

☐ is fine as it is.

☐ causes no problems.

☐ makes parents pierce themselves.

96 True, false or not in the text?

	true	false	not in the text
a Body piercing is the latest fashion for teenagers.	☐	☐	☐
b It can be dangerous to pierce your body yourself.	☐	☐	☐
c There are many shops specialised in piercing all over the UK.	☐	☐	☐
d There is no law about body piercing in the UK.	☐	☐	☐
e You can do body piercing to adults only.	☐	☐	☐
f To get a real 'tattoo' you'll have to wait till you're 18.	☐	☐	☐
g A 'smile gem' is a diamond stuck on the ears.	☐	☐	☐

Language

97 Complete the mind map.

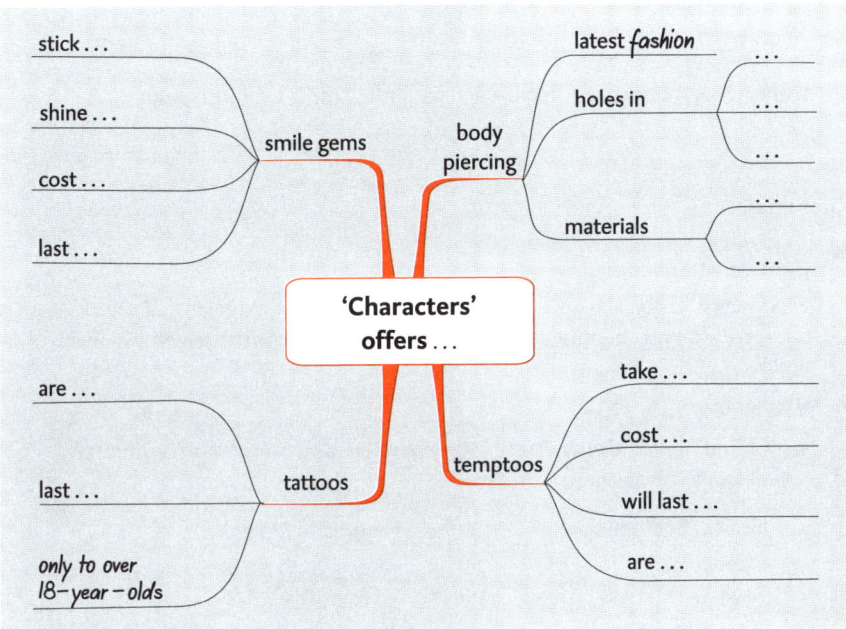

98 Match the clothes and accessories on the left with the correct part of the body (there is one more accessory than you need).

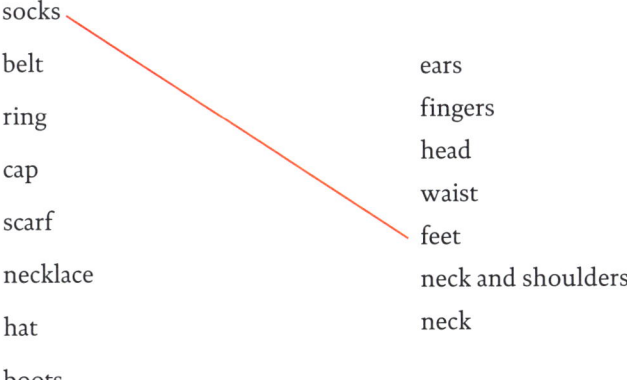

socks

belt   ears

ring   fingers

cap   head

scarf   waist

necklace   feet

hat   neck and shoulders

boots   neck

99 Put the parts of the sentences into the correct order.

  a already / Have / for the body piercing / made an appointment /
next Friday / you?

      _____

  b time / No, / because / have / I / haven't / didn't / I / enough.

      _____

Grammatik

> **_if-clause_ – Der Bedingungssatz**
>
> Bedingungssätze im Englischen werden **durch das Wort _if_ eingeleitet**. Damit kannst
> du sagen, was unter bestimmten Bedingungen geschieht, was passieren kann oder was
> nötig ist.
>
> **Wie bildest du _if_-Sätze?**
>
> - Im **_if_-Teil** wird die **Gegenwart** (_simple present_) und im **Hauptsatz** die **Zukunft**
>   (_will-future_) gebraucht.
>
> | _if_-Satz (Bedingung) | Hauptsatz (Folge) |
> | --- | --- |
> | If you hurry, | you will catch the bus. |
> | Gegenwart (_simple present_) | Zukunft (_will-future_) |
> | _Wenn du dich beeilst,_ | _dann erwischst du den Bus (noch)._ |
>
> Der _if_-Satz kann auch nach dem Hauptsatz stehen, z. B.: You will catch the bus if you
>   hurry.
>
> - Im Hauptsatz kann statt des **_will-future_** auch **can + Grundform**, **must + Grundform**
>   oder die **Befehlsform** stehen.
>   _Beispiele:_ If you want to find something out, you can go to the library. _(can + Grundform)_
>   If you like old churches, you must visit St. Paul's Cathedral. _(must + Grundform)_
>   If you have any problems, give me a ring! _(Befehlsform)_
>
> - Hauptsatz und _if_-Satz können auch **verneint** sein.
>   _Beispiele:_ If it doesn't rain, we will go for a walk in the park.
>   If it rains, we won't go there.
>   If it doesn't rain, you won't need an umbrella.
>
> **Beachte:** In dem Teil des Satzes, der _if_ enthält, darf _will_ nicht vorkommen!
> Eine Eselsbrücke: **'If' and 'will' makes teachers ill.**

100 Match the beginnings and endings of the sentences.
Mrs Lemmon is talking to her daughter, Sarah.

A   If you play with knives,   (1)   you'll miss the train.
B   If you work hard,   (2)   you'll cut yourself.
C   If you don't stop eating sweets,   (3)   I'll always be there for you.
D   If you take these pills,   (4)   you'll pass your exams.
E   If you need help,   (5)   you'll feel better soon.
F   If you don't hurry up,   (6)   you'll get bad teeth.

A	B	C	D	E	F

101 Get to know more about Sarah Lemmon's plans and her situation.
Complete the sentences with these phrases.

she ⟨ will / won't ⟩ get   save   go   eat   pay   leave   miss   buy

a   If Sarah has time on Saturday, _____ shopping.

b   If Sarah has enough money for trendy shoes, _____ some.

c   If it starts to rain, _____ to the beach.

d   If she feels hungry, _____ a sandwich.

e   If her mother can't find her credit card, _____ cash.

f   If Sarah repairs her bike herself, _____ money.

g   If she sells old toys at a flea market, _____ some money.

h   If Sarah doesn't hurry, _____ the bus.

Text Production

102 What do you say?

a Sage, dass du dir ein Piercing machen lassen
wirst, wenn deine Eltern es erlauben.

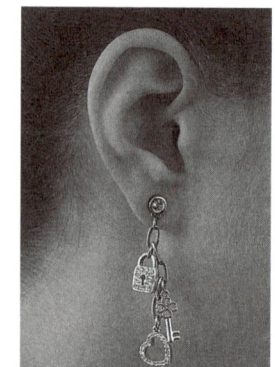

_____

_____

b Erzähle, dass deine Freundin Caro keine
smile gems kaufen durfte.

_____

_____

c Stelle fest, dass dauerhafte *tattoos* nicht ideal für junge Leute sind.

_____

103 E-Mail
Beachte: Deine E-Mail sollte mindestens 10 Sätze umfassen.
Achte auf die richtige Zeit.

Angaben zur Empfängerin: Deine Freundin Sarah (17) aus Cambridge hatte
großen Streit mit ihren Eltern, weil sie sich gegen deren Willen ein Zungenpiercing machen lassen will. Sie überlegt, sich selbst wenigstens am Ohr zu
piercen.

- Bedanke dich für ihre E-Mail.
- Erkläre, dass du Sarah gut verstehen kannst und noch eine Freundin hast,
  die auch ein Zungenpiercing haben möchte. Berichte, dass auch deren Eltern
  es nicht erlauben, solange sie nicht 18 ist.
- Rate Sarah, lieber bis zu ihrem 18. Geburtstag zu warten. Schreibe, dass du
  wegen des Piercings keinen Streit mit deinen Eltern anfangen würdest.
- Frage, warum Sarah wegen der Ohrlöcher nicht in ein Geschäft geht, das auf
  body piercing spezialisiert ist.
- Sage deutlich deine Meinung, dass du dich nicht selbst am Ohr piercen
  würdest! Berichte, dass du in einer Jugendzeitschrift gelesen hast, dass es
  sehr gefährlich sein und zu einer Blutvergiftung führen kann, wenn Teen-
  ager sich selbst piercen.

- Beschreibe deine Zukunftsträume, was du alles tun würdest, wenn du schon 18 wärst, z. B. dass du mit 18 Jahren gern eine eigene kleine Wohnung haben würdest und dass du auch gern ein eigenes Haustier (am liebsten …) hättest.
- Bedaure, dass du Sarah nicht helfen konntest, und tröste sie, dass auch du noch immer deine Eltern fragen musst, wenn du z. B. ausgehen willst.
- Erkläre, dass du oft mit deinen Eltern diskutierst und du mit deiner Mutter deine Probleme besprechen kannst.
- Drücke die Hoffnung aus, dass Sarah mit ihren Eltern in Zukunft gut auskommen wird.
- Bitte Sarah, bald zurückzuschreiben und auch ihre Eltern zu grüßen.

Checkpoint

Dieses Kapitel ist ein **Test** für dich: Es enthält Übungen zu allen grammatischen Themen, die im Kapitel *Topics and tasks* behandelt werden. Du hast zwei Möglichkeiten:

▶ Du kannst den Test als Erstes durcharbeiten, um festzustellen, ob du die in der 9. Klasse behandelte Grammatik beherrschst.

▶ Du kannst zuerst die einzelnen *topics* durcharbeiten und danach den Test machen.

Wenn du mit einer Aufgabe Schwierigkeiten hast, solltest du das **Grammatik-thema wiederholen**. Damit du die Stelle im Buch, an der das Grammatik-thema erklärt wird, schneller findest, stehen **im Lösungsteil** *Key* bei den Auf-gaben entsprechende **Verweise**.

104 Comparisons – interesting facts and world records.

a Alaska is _____ (cold) Florida.

b Antarctica is _____ (cold) place in the world.

c Death Valley is _____ (hot) place in the USA.

d Mont Blanc is _____ (high) mountain in Europe.

e Mount Everest is _____ (high) Mont Blanc.

f The Nile is _____ (long) river in the world.

g The river Rhine is _____ (long) the river Thames.

h Washington is _____ (small) New York.

i London is _____ (big) Edinburgh.

j The Mona Lisa is _____ (famous) painting in the world.

105 Comparisons – personal experiences.

   a   My father is _____ *(genauso alt wie)* my mother.

   b   What do you think? Is stealing _____
        (schlechter / schlimmer als) telling lies?

   c   This year my English teacher is very pleased because my English is
        _____ *(nicht so schlecht wie)* last year.

   d   I find maths _____ *(nicht so schwierig wie)* physics.

   e   My new mountain bike was _____ *(teurer als)* yours.

   f   I think the Queen is one of _____ *(reichsten)* persons in
        the world.

   g   For me Euro Disney is _____ *(großartigste)* tourist
        attraction in Paris.

   h   That was _____ *(schlechteste)* book I've ever read.

   i   Titanic is _____ *(beste)* Hollywood film I've ever seen.

   j   It's _____ *(schwierigste)* exam I've ever taken.

106 Michael Brown is planning a party next weekend.

   a   If Michael's parents let him, he _____ (have) 50 guests
        at he party.

   b   He wonders whether his friends _____ (bring) him any
        presents.

   c   Michael is good at organising things and he _____
        (not make) any mistakes in planning his party.

   d   Mr Brown, Michael's father _____ (not be) at
        the party on Saturday.

   e   He is on a business trip to London so he _____
        (not celebrate) Michael's birthday with him.

107 Translate.

a Wird das Wetter morgen schön?

_____

b Es wird morgen wahrscheinlich regnen.

_____

c Wenn es regnet, wird die Party im Haus sein.

_____

d Sie hat genug Geld gespart. Sie wird sich bald ein neues Auto kaufen.

_____

_____

e Wenn du betrunken Auto fährst, wirst du deinen Führerschein *(driving licence)* verlieren.

_____

_____

f Wenn du regelmäßig Sport treibst, wirst du fit bleiben.

_____

_____

_____

_____

_____

108 Test your tenses. Tom and Michael, old friends, meet again and ask each other a lot of questions.

a _____ (leave) school yet?

Yes, I have.

b _____ (ever visit) Australia?

No, I've never been there.

c But I _____ (go) to Florida and California last summer.

d How much _____ (pay) for your trip to the USA?

Oh, it was terribly expensive, but my parents were very helpful.

e _____ (see) our old friend Claire recently?

Yes, I _____ (meet) her yesterday evening at her apartment.

f Imagine – she _____ (prepare) a five-course-meal for me yesterday.

g The meal _____ (be) delicious last night.

h I _____ (come) home very late last Friday.

i Oh, look! I _____ (just get) another message from her.

j That's ten messages today. I think she _____ (fall in love) with me.

109 Tom knows a lot about Claire. Find the correct ending.

At the moment …	… she jogs in the park.
Last year …	… she was bullied by her classmates because she always wore unfashionable clothes.
She hopes …	… she has wanted to be a Hollywood actress.
Every morning …	… she's doing her exercises at the fitness studio.
When she was a schoolgirl …	… she got a job with a drama company.
Since she was young …	… she'll act in a famous musical one day.

110 Test your conjunctions. Pete is writing to Pamela.

> and – both – so – as long as – but – because – although

I've arrived in London safely and the weather is really nice. It's _____ warm _____ sunny. _____ my hotel is quite cheap it's in the centre and close to an underground station. I had to take a room without a private bathroom _____ it was the only one left. You can also get Wi-Fi access at the hotel _____ you are a guest there. I want to write some e-mails, _____ I've forgotten my address book. Could you look for it? Please bring it with you. The sights are great _____ don't forget your new camera.

111 Find the right conjunctions.

> so – ever since – in order to – as if – as soon as – but – because – as long as

a It looks _____ it will rain soon.

b We had to put on the heating _____ it was a very cold day.

c I have saved enough money _____ I can now afford to buy a digital camera.

d I've worked for this company _____ I left university.

e You can have a garden party _____ the neighbours don't complain about the noise.

f You can go skating _____ you finish your homework.

g I worked very hard _____ pass my exams.

h He smiled _____ he didn't say a word.

112 Pronouns – choose the correct words.

a (my – an – his)
I have _____ own mountain bike now.

b (be me – myself – mine)
I paid for it _____.

c (my – mine – myself)
Your mountain bike was cheaper than _____.

d (his – himself – her)
John had an accident, he broke _____ arm.

e (him – himself – his)
Have you repaired John's bike? – No, he can do it _____.

f (you – yourself – yours)
Will you clean my bike? – No, I won't. Clean it _____.

g (me – my – mine – myself)

If you don't clean _____ bike, I'll clean it _____.

h (theirs – their – them)

In the evening the other cyclists often forget to take _____

lights with _____.

i (us – ourselves – we)

John and I often go to mountain bike races and today Mary came with

_____. We all enjoy _____ very much.

j (him – his – he)

John's brother is a great mountain biker. Look at _____.

_____ really cycles fast. _____ will be the best time.

113 Complete the sentences.

a (you – like travel)   (enjoy this book)

　If you like travelling, you'll enjoy this book.

b (you – look in the telephone directory)   (find my number)

_____

c (I – not know the meaning of a word)   (use a dictionary)

_____

d (you – feed the animals)   (zoo attendant – be very angry)

_____

e (Tom – need advice)   (talk to a teacher)

_____

f (I – not go swimming)   (it's too cold)

_____

g (you – book a flight last-minute)   (get it cheaper)

_____

h (you – can't speak English)   (not get the job)

_____

i (I – promise to drive carefully)   (let me borrow your motorbike?)

_____

114 Rewrite these sentences using an adverb instead of an adjective.

a Susan is a bad tennis player.
Susan plays tennis <u>badly</u>.

b But she is a wonderful dancer.
She dances _____.

c Her brother is a slow worker.
He works _____.

d But he is a careful driver.
But he drives _____.

e Susan and her brother aren't quick learners.
They _____.

f But they are good piano players.
They play the piano _____.

Vocabulary

Unter **Vocabulary** findest du schwierige Wörter, die in diesem Buch vorkommen.

▶ Du kannst die Liste verwenden, um unbekannte **Wörter nachzuschlagen**, die dir in den Texten oder Übungen begegnen.

▶ Du kannst mit der Liste aber auch deinen **Wortschatz erweitern:** Nimm dir jeden Tag einige Wörter (5–10) vor und lerne sie. Setze die gelernten Wörter dann im Unterricht oder im Kontakt mit englischsprachigen Freunden ein.

Der Abschnitt **Irregular verbs** enthält eine Liste mit den wichtigsten unregelmäßigen Verben. Diese Liste kannst du zum Nachschlagen verwenden oder zum regelmäßigen Üben der unregelmäßigen Verbformen.

Vocabulary

Aa
(to) accuse someone	jemanden anklagen
actually	wirklich, tatsächlich
advice	Rat
amazing	erstaunlich, verblüffend
(to) appear	erscheinen
area	Fläche
as soon as	sobald
attention	Aufmerksamkeit

Bb
beef	Rindfleisch
beef fat	Rinderfett
beef flavour	Rindfleischaroma, Rindfleischgeschmack
(to) believe	glauben
(to) blame someone	jemandem die Schuld geben/verantwortlich machen
(to) bully	terrorisieren

Cc
(to) celebrate	feiern
certainly	gewiss, sicher
chain	Kette
(to) change	ändern
choice	(Aus-)Wahl
circle	Kreis
clothing	Bekleidung
confident	selbstbewusst, zuversichtlich
(to) cover	bedecken

Dd
damage	Schaden
(to) dare	wagen, sich trauen
(to) decide	entscheiden
deliberate	bewusst, absichtlich
(to) disappear	verschwinden
disease	Krankheit
during	während

Ee	earthquake	Erdbeben
	either … or	entweder … oder
	everyone	jeder, alle
	excited	aufgeregt
	(to) expand	sich ausweiten

Ff	fact	Tatsache
	fame	Ruhm
	fantasy	Einbildungskraft
	fault	Fehler
	favourite	Lieblings-
	feature	Merkmal, (Haupt-)Attraktion
	flavour	Geschmack, Aroma
	(to) focus on sth.	sich konzentrieren auf etw.
	former	früher, ehemalig
	fried	gebraten
	fries	eigentlich *French fried potatoes*: Pommes frites

Gg	gem	Edelstein
	gossip	Geschwätz, Gerede
	greenhouse effect	Treibhauseffekt
	ground	Erdboden

Hh	habit	Gewohnheit
	(to) hide	sich verstecken
	hole	Loch
	holy	heilig

Ii	immediately	sofort
	in order to	um … zu
	(to) include	einschließen
	(to) increase	anwachsen, zunehmen
	instead of	an Stelle von

Jj	jealous	eifersüchtig
	(to) join	verbinden, verknüpfen
	journey	Reise
	judge	(Preis-)Richter*in

Kk	kind	Art, Sorte
	kindly (adv.)	freundlich
Ll	(to) last four weeks	vier Wochen dauern
	law	Gesetz
	likely	wahrscheinlich, voraussichtlich
Mm	(to) melt	schmelzen
	(to) mislead someone	jemanden täuschen, irreführen
Nn	nail	(Finger-)Nagel
	nearly	beinahe, fast
	neither … nor	weder … noch
Oo	(to) overcome	überwinden
Pp	participant	Teilnehmer*in
	(to) participate	teilnehmen, mitmachen
	particularly	besonders
	(to) pierce	durchbohren
	poisoning	Vergiftung
	possession	Besitztum, Eigentum
	powder	Puder
	(to) pray	beten
	(to) prepare	vorbereiten
	prison	Gefängnis
Qq	quite	ziemlich, recht
Rr	(to) receive	erhalten
	relationship	Beziehung
	(to) rescue	retten
	(to) rise	sich erheben, ansteigen
	rough	rau
Ss	(to) search	suchen
	security	Sicherheit
	self-conscious	befangen, gehemmt
	smart	gepflegt, elegant; intelligent

	(to) smile	lächeln
	spectator	Zuschauer*in
	(to) spread	sich ausbreiten
	stage	Bühne
	(to) stick	festkleben
	strict	streng
	success	Erfolg
Tt	(to) tease	ärgern
	terrible	schrecklich, furchtbar, fürchterlich
	tongue	Zunge
	trouble	Mühe, Last, Schwierigkeit
	truth	Wahrheit
Uu	unlike	unähnlich, verschieden
	unthinkable	unvorstellbar, undenkbar
	used	gebraucht
	(to) be used to	gewöhnt sein an
	usual	üblich, gewöhnlich
Vv	voice	Stimme
Ww	wave	Welle
	(to) wipe	(weg)wischen
	worried	beunruhigt, ängstlich

Irregular verbs

Grundform	1. Vergangenheit	Partizip Perfekt	deutsche Übersetzung
(to) be	was/were	been	*sein*
(to) beat	beat	beaten	*schlagen*
(to) become	became	become	*werden*
(to) begin	began	begun	*beginnen*
(to) break	broke	broken	*brechen*
(to) bring	brought	brought	*bringen*
(to) build	built	built	*bauen*
(to) buy	bought	bought	*kaufen*
(to) catch	caught	caught	*fangen*
(to) choose	chose	chosen	*wählen*
(to) come	came	come	*kommen*
(to) cost	cost	cost	*kosten*
(to) cut	cut	cut	*schneiden*
(to) do	did	done	*tun*
(to) draw	drew	drawn	*zeichnen, ziehen*
(to) dream	dreamt/ed	dreamt/ed	*träumen*
(to) drink	drank	drunk	*trinken*
(to) drive	drove	driven	*fahren*
(to) eat	ate	eaten	*essen*
(to) fall	fell	fallen	*fallen*
(to) feed	fed	fed	*füttern*
(to) feel	felt	felt	*fühlen*
(to) fight	fought	fought	*kämpfen*
(to) find	found	found	*finden*
(to) fly	flew	flown	*fliegen*
(to) forget	forgot	forgotten	*vergessen*
(to) forgive	forgave	forgiven	*vergeben*
(to) get	got	got	*bekommen*
(to) give	gave	given	*geben*
(to) go	went	gone	*gehen*
(to) grow	grew	grown	*wachsen*
(to) have	had	had	*haben*
(to) hear	heard	heard	*hören*
(to) hide	hid	hidden	*verstecken*
(to) hit	hit	hit	*treffen, schlagen*
(to) hurt	hurt	hurt	*verletzen*

Grundform	1. Vergangenheit	Partizip Perfekt	deutsche Übersetzung
(to) keep	kept	kept	*halten*
(to) know	knew	known	*wissen*
(to) lay	laid	laid	*legen*
(to) learn	learnt/ed	learnt/ed	*lernen*
(to) leave	left	left	*verlassen*
(to) lie	lay	lain	*liegen*
(to) lose	lost	lost	*verlieren*
(to) make	made	made	*machen*
(to) mean	meant	meant	*meinen, bedeuten*
(to) meet	met	met	*treffen*
(to) pay	paid	paid	*bezahlen*
(to) put	put	put	*setzen, stellen, legen*
(to) read	read	read	*lesen*
(to) ring	rang	rung	*läuten*
(to) run	ran	run	*laufen, rennen*
(to) say	said	said	*sagen*
(to) see	saw	seen	*sehen*
(to) sell	sold	sold	*verkaufen*
(to) send	sent	sent	*senden*
(to) show	showed	shown	*zeigen*
(to) shut	shut	shut	*schließen*
(to) sing	sang	sung	*singen*
(to) sit	sat	sat	*sitzen*
(to) sleep	slept	slept	*schlafen*
(to) speak	spoke	spoken	*sprechen*
(to) spell	spelt	spelt	*buchstabieren*
(to) spend	spent	spent	*verbringen, ausgeben*
(to) stand	stood	stood	*stehen*
(to) swim	swam	swum	*schwimmen*
(to) take	took	taken	*nehmen*
(to) teach	taught	taught	*lehren*
(to) tell	told	told	*erzählen*
(to) think	thought	thought	*denken, glauben*
(to) throw	threw	thrown	*werfen*
(to) understand	understood	understood	*verstehen*
(to) wear	wore	worn	*tragen*
(to) win	won	won	*gewinnen*
(to) write	wrote	written	*schreiben*

Key

Dieses Kapitel enthält die Lösungen zu allen Aufgaben. Damit du sie schneller findest, wurden viele der Lösungen **fett hervorgehoben**. Beachte, dass es oft mehr als nur eine einzige richtige Lösung gibt. Die verschiedenen Lösungsmöglichkeiten sind durch Schrägstriche voneinander getrennt, in Klammern stehende Wörter oder Satzteile können entfallen.

Die Lösungen zur Textproduktion sind als Vorschlag zu verstehen. Lass dich deshalb nicht entmutigen, wenn deine Lösung von der hier angegebenen abweicht!

Prüfe bitte auch deine Rechtschreibung genau. Wenn deine Lösung falsch war, solltest du die Übung später noch einmal wiederholen.

Topic 1: Carnivals around the world

1 Tick (✓) the right answer.

a The Notting Hill Carnival started ...

☐ over fifty years ago.

☐ less than ten years ago.

✓ over thirty-five years ago.

☐ less than twenty years ago.

b The groups at the Notting Hill Carnival come ...

☐ just from England.

✓ from all over the world.

☐ just from the Caribbean.

☐ from all over Europe.

c How many 'Sound Systems' are there at the Notting Hill Carnival?

✓ over fifty

☐ a million

☐ just three

☐ about a hundred

d The largest carnival on Earth takes place in ...

☐ London.

☐ Germany.

☐ Trinidad.

✓ Brazil.

e At the Rio Carnival the judges see each samba school for about ...

☐ two nights.

✓ 90 minutes.

☐ ten hours.

☐ twelve hours.

f At Carnival time in Rio everything . . .

- [ ] costs the same as usual.
- [ ] is cheaper than usual.
- [ ] is a little more expensive than usual.
- [✓] is much more expensive than usual.

2 True, false or not in the text?

	true	false	not in the text
a Notting Hill is in Trinidad.		✓	
b The film *Notting Hill* is about the carnival.		✓	
c Notting Hill Carnival is in the summer.	✓		
d The weather in Rio is very hot at carnival.			✓
e The samba schools spend two days preparing for the Rio Carnival.		✓	
f The Rio Carnival is very noisy.	✓		

3
a The Notting Hill Carnival is multi-cultural **because** groups from all over the world take part.
b People visit Carnival in Rio de Janeiro **although** it's very expensive.
c Carnival in Rio is famous all over the world **but** Europe's largest carnival isn't well-known.
d Tourists can follow one of the parades **or** listen to the music from three live stages.

4
a ~~wood~~ → tools
b ~~Russian~~ → countries / states, nations
c ~~teach~~ → occupations / jobs
d ~~Germany~~ → languages
e ~~housewife~~ → relatives / family members

5
a great
b enjoy
c eager
d everything
e district

6

amazing	**more amazing**	(the) most amazing
pretty	**prettier**	(the) prettiest
expensive	**more expensive**	**(the) most expensive**
fantastic	more fantastic	**(the) most fantastic**
quiet	**quieter**	**(the) quietest**
noisy	**noisier**	**(the) noisiest**
important	more important	**(the) most important**
elegant	**more elegant**	**(the) most elegant**
spectacular	**more spectacular**	**(the) most spectacular**
large	**larger**	(the) largest

7
- a A plane is **faster** than a car.
- b A horror film is **more exciting** than a documentary film.
- c Walking is **slower** than in-line skating.
- d Commercials are **funnier** than news.
- e A trip to New York is **more expensive** than a flight to London.

8
- a nicer than
- b bigger than
- c as loud as / louder than
- d most spectacular
- e best
- f higher than
- g more expensive than
- h the most exciting
- i more amazing costumes than

9
- a I think (that) / In my opinion / I believe (that) / I guess (that), *Notting Hill* is the best romantic film.
- b Can you / Could you / Would you tell us about the film?
- c Do you know (about) / Have you ever heard of the Carnival in Cologne?
- d I think (that) / In my opinion / I believe (that) / I guess (that) the Carnival in Cologne is the greatest street party in Germany.

10

Dear Anne and Mark,

Thank you for your e-mail and the invitation to London.
I'd love to come to London to visit you! I spent a week in London last year with my parents and I enjoyed it very much. We took a sightseeing tour on a double-decker bus. I saw Buckingham Palace, the Tower of London, Trafalgar Square, St. Paul's Cathedral and a lot more, but I've never been to Notting Hill.
How often have you been to the Notting Hill Carnival? I don't know very much about it. Where do the participants and the spectators come from? What parts of the Carnival do you like best? What do people wear at the Carnival and what's the food like?
I'm surprised that London has such an event. Where does the Notting Hill Carnival originally come from?
Could you send me a link about Notting Hill Carnival? That would be great.
It's a pity that I've never seen the film 'Notting Hill'. But recently I've seen a fantastic … film called '…' with … – I enjoyed it very much.

Please write back soon!

Yours …

Topic 2: Global Warming

11 Tick (✓) the right answer.

  a The 'greenhouse effect' means that in winter
the weather in Europe will be …

    [✓] drier.

    [ ] colder.

    [ ] the same.

    [ ] wetter.

  b The area of ground which has permafrost in Russia is …

    [ ] less than half the country.

    [✓] getting smaller.

    [ ] 250 kilometres wide.

    [ ] getting bigger.

  c Permafrost is useful because you can …

    [✓] store food in it.

    [ ] grow food in it.

    [ ] cook food in it.

    [ ] find food in it.

  d In the USA the idea that the sea will cover the east coast cities is …

    [✓] a horror movie.

    [ ] getting warmer.

    [ ] getting much more likely.

    [ ] rising.

  e Global warming will create …

    [ ] new diseases.

    [✓] the spread of diseases.

    [ ] fewer diseases.

    [ ] diseases which kill mosquitoes.

f In Japan global warming will ...

☐ cause earthquakes.

☐ make volcanoes erupt.

☐ cause tidal waves.

☑ make the sea rise.

g In Japan global warming will ...

☑ make millions of people homeless.

☐ make life in Tokyo and Osaka easier.

☐ get millions of people to live below sea level.

☐ make life for people much better.

		true	false
12	**a** There'll be more flooding all over Europe because of global warming.	☑	☐
	b More than half of the ground in Russia is covered by 'permafrost'.	☑	☐
	c The 'permafrost' in Russia hasn't started to melt yet.	☐	☑
	d In the USA the greenhouse effect will make the sea expand and change the climate.	☑	☐
	e The spread of diseases will be another effect of rising temperatures all over the world.	☑	☐
	f Africa produces more CO_2 than Great Britain.	☐	☑
	g Only a few people in Japan live below sea level, so global warming won't have effects on them.	☐	☑

13

Europe	Russia: melting 'permafrost'	Africa
wetter **autumns** and winters	**houses** will fall down	more **food** shortages
drier **summers**	the **permafrost** will melt	more **floods**
longer periods without **rain**	roads will **disappear**	malaria will spread to new **areas**

14
a Hitze
b verändern
c Jahrhundert
d Überschwemmungen / Überflutungen
e Gebiete / Flächen
f verlassen
g Gesundheitsprobleme
h zunehmen, anwachsen

15

noun	adjective
danger	dangerous
health	**healthy**
warmth	warm
length	long

16
a a <u>short</u> distance   → a **long** distance
b <u>above</u> sea level   → **below** sea level
c **bad** weather   → <u>fine</u> weather
d the <u>first</u> time   → the **last** time
e **low** temperatures   → <u>high</u> temperatures
f an <u>easy</u> question   → a **difficult** question
g a **global** /**international** problem   → a <u>local</u> problem
h <u>ask</u> a question   → **answer** a question
i **dry** weather   → <u>wet</u> weather

17
a buildings: houses, skyscrapers, towers
b continents: Africa, Australia, Europe, America, Asia
c weather conditions: rain, storm, sunshine, hail, snowfall, …
d natural catastrophes: tidal waves, earthquakes, typhoons, …

18
a volcanoes, earthquakes, typhoons, ~~coasts~~
b ~~Europe~~, New York, Boston, Tokyo
c storms, floods, ~~temperatures~~, typhoons
d atmosphere, gas, CO_2, ~~century~~

19
a child – **until** – wild – night – ride
b keep – heat – people – disease – **health** – mean
c coast – close – **flood** – also – roads – whole
d rise – like – dry – price – **insects** – railway lines
e **country** – allow – down – round – houses – found

20
a The 'greenhouse effect' will change the world.
b There will be more flooding in Europe.
c Even in the USA diseases will spread.
d There will be more food shortage in Africa.
e In Japan millions of people will leave their homes.
f Health problems will increase all over the world.

21
a **Where** are there many volcanoes? – In Japan.
b **How many** people live under sea level in Tokyo? – Millions!
c **Why** is global warming dangerous for Africa? – Because there will be more floods, more food shortage and more diseases.
d **Who** produces as much CO_2 as the whole of Africa? – Britain.

22 Tomorrow it **will be cloudy** in Scotland with **rain** and **strong** winds. In the Midlands it **will be** mainly **dry** with light **winds**. In the south of Great Britain it **will be sunny** with **light winds**.

23
a If Sandra's parents let her, she **will have** a party.
b If her Dad allows it, Sandra **will use** her father's car to go shopping for her party.
c She hopes nobody **will bring** alcoholic drinks to her party.
d Sandra hopes a lot of people from her class **will come** to the pary.
e If it rains, they **will take** the bus.
f If John promises not to come late, they **will wait** for him.
g John's sister **will get** very angry if she sees him eating all her chocolates at the party.

24

Dear Thomas,

Thank you for your long e-mail and the invitation to Edinburgh.
I'll visit you as soon as possible. I'll bring my friend Peter with me. (I'm looking forward to bringing my friend Peter with me.) We'll start to save money for the flight.
At school I'll work on a project: I'll use the internet to find out about the greenhouse effect and design a poster for my class.
You know, the greenhouse effect means that gases like carbon dioxide keep heat in the atmosphere: Europe will be warmer in the future with drier summers and longer periods without rain. There will also be wetter autumns and winters!
I'm sure there will be more floods all over the world.
Will you talk about the greenhouse effect at school, too? I don't think that people will stop global warming in the future.
But I hope the doctors will stop the spread of diseases.

I hope you'll write back soon. Give my regards to your parents,

Yours …

Topic 3: Beef in Fries?

25 Tick (✓) the right answer.

a Hindus in America ...

☐ don't have any problems with food.

☐ like to eat steaks.

☐ like to eat horses.

☑ are not allowed to eat beef.

b Before 1990 Mr Sharma ...

☐ often went to a McDonald's restaurant.

☐ ate hamburgers.

☐ ate cheeseburgers.

☑ didn't eat at Mc Donald's.

c After 1990 Mr Sharma began to eat McDonald's French fries because ...

☑ he believed they were vegetarian.

☐ he had enough money.

☐ he liked the taste of the oil.

☐ everyone else did.

d McDonald's ...

☐ cooked their French fries in beef fat.

☐ cooked their French fries in the factory.

☐ used beef fat and vegetable oil to cook French fries.

☑ flavoured French fries with beef in the factory.

e Mr Sharma said that the mistake was ...

☐ a friend's.

☐ his.

☑ McDonald's.

☐ no-one's.

f Walt Riker said that the fault was ...

☐ McDonald's.

☐ the vegetarian restaurant's.

☑ not McDonald's.

☐ the market's.

g When Mahendra Jagirdar heard about the fries he ...

☑ stopped going to McDonald's.

☐ became a vegetarian.

☐ went to India.

☐ became an engineer.

26 **a** Mr Sharma is a **Hindu**.
   d He **works** for Boeing in Seattle.
   c He never went **to a McDonald's restaurant** before 1990.
   d He began going to McDonald's to eat **French fries**.
   e He was **shocked** when he read the news about beef in fries.
   f He accuses McDonald's of misleading **its customers**.
   g He is looking for ways to **clean himself**.

27

A	B	C	D
3	1	2	5

28 **a** I like to eat **out**.
   b Do you like **to** go to fast-food restaurants?
   c Do you prefer a simple café **to** a big restaurant?
   d I'm very fond **of** Italian food.
   e I hate to wash **up** the dishes. Let's leave the kitchen!
   f Shall we call a taxi or go **by** tube?
   g I'm hungry. What's **on** the menu today?
   h Can you ask **for** the menu, please?
   i Oh, look, the menu is lying over there **in front of** the mirror. I can get it myself.
   j I looked **at** the menu and found some vegetarian dishes.
   k Would you put the menu **in** the cupboard, please?

29

Mercury, Mars, Venus	planets
Buddhism, Hinduism, Christianity	**religions**
Australia, Asia, Europe	**continents**
Atlantic, Pacific, Indian	**oceans**
Swiss, American, Italian	**nationalities**
lipstick, mascara, eye-liner	**make-up**
penicilin, morphine, codeine	**drugs**

30

A TV programme — producer
A restaurant — manager
A school — headteacher
A football team — captain
A group of workers — foreperson
A company — managing director
A choir — choir leader
A pet shop — shop keeper

31

A	B	C	D	E	F	G
4	5	6	1	7	2	3

32

a Teacher: 'Susie, are these headphones **yours**?'
Susie: 'Yes, they're **mine**.'

b Teacher: 'Sarah and Fatma: Are the smartphones **yours**?'
Sarah and Fatma: 'Yes, they're **ours**.'

c Teacher: 'Robert says it is **his** / **yours**. Is that true?'
John: 'No, it is Peggy's ball. Yes, I'm sure the basketball is **hers**.'

d Teacher: 'Where are Liz and Peter? Here are two exercise books.'
John: 'They're at the gym. But I know the exercise books are **theirs**. Look at the names.'

e John: 'I've found a bag of sweets. Is it **yours**?'
Michael: 'No, ask the girls. Perhaps it's **theirs**.'
John: 'OK, but if nobody owns it, the bag of sweets is **mine**!'

f John: 'Mr White, I've found these old trainers.
Are they **yours**?'
Teacher: 'Let me see – Yes, of course they're **mine**!'

33 The Sharmas' new home

Mr Sharma and his family moved to a new house because they had to leave **their** apartment. Asif and **his** little brother got a big room on the first floor.

They decorated the room **themselves**. 'Can you help **us** to carry the computer upstairs?' the boys asked Mr Sharma. 'Oh, you don't need **me**, it isn't heavy, you can carry it **yourselves**!' he answered. 'Here are some computer games, Asif. Are they **yours**?' Mr Sharma asked. 'Yes, they're **mine / ours**,' **his** son answered. 'Have a break! Would **you** like a piece of cheesecake?' Mrs Sharma asked. 'I prepared it **myself** in **my / our** new oven.'

'Great, I love cheesecake,' Asif answered, ran into the kitchen and took the sharp knife carelessly. He tried to cut the cake and hurt **himself**. **His** mother got some plaster from **her** handbag and put it round **his** bleeding finger. Poor Asif.

Now they all have tea and cheesecake. '**Our** new home is great. We'll enjoy **ourselves** here, I'm sure, as we have more room for **us** all now.'

34

It's your body – get fit and check your diet!

Nowadays a lot of young people have an unhealthy lifestyle. They/We …
- eat unhealthy food.
- eat in a hurry, standing in a fast-food restaurant.
- eat too much junk food with lots of fat und sugar.
- are not active in our free time.
- don't do a lot of sport.

How do you stay fit? Do you do sport?

Or do you prefer watching TV, surfing the Internet or playing video games? My hobby is in-line skating. I often practise after school. And I learn cooking at the youth club.

Have you ever tried
- badminton?
- abseiling?
- jogging?
- judo?

Come to the **youth club** and meet active young people. Learn a lot about healthy food and perfect cooking here.

Do more sport,
watch your diet,
stay fit and active.
It's your body – look after yourself.

Topic 4: Star Problem

35 Tick (✓) the right answer.

a Pete thinks the class bullied him because …

☐ of his name.

☑ he was on TV.

☐ he was good at sport.

☐ he was in Year 9.

b Pete …

☑ never found out exactly why the class decided to bully him.

☐ knew exactly why the class decided to bully him.

☐ didn't know the names of the bullies.

☐ was jealous of the other people in the class.

c The class bullied Pete …

☐ when he was on TV.

☐ only when he was at school.

☐ only out of school.

☑ at school, out of school and during exams.

d Because of the bullying Pete …

☑ didn't want to go to school any more.

☐ found that his schoolwork got worse and worse.

☐ was on TV more often.

☐ made some new friends.

e After Pete saw the Head …

☐ he felt terrible.

☐ he went to another school.

☑ he studied in a room on his own.

☐ he was in a room next to his mother.

f When school began again after the summer holiday ...

- ☐ everyone bullied Pete.
- ☑ no-one bullied Pete.
- ☐ his mum and teacher talked to Pete.
- ☐ no-one talked to Pete.

g Pete thinks that bullying ...

- ☐ happens to everyone.
- ☐ only happens to people who are on TV.
- ☐ happens to people who talk to the teacher.
- ☑ can happen to anyone.

36

a His classmates **bullied** Pete.

b **Everyone** in Pete's class called him names.

e Pete's **teacher** took him to see the Head.

37

a Almost overnight everyone in the class **started bullying** Pete.

b The bullies were **jealous** of Pete being on TV.

c Pete was shocked that some of the bullies **were** his friends.

d The more Pete was on TV the **more** they bullied him.

e Pete never **knew** / **found** out why they decided to bully him.

f He felt glad that he **told** / **talked to** his mum and teacher.

g Talking **helped** with his problems.

38

a
- ☑ One of them was badly injured.
- ☐ Bullies hurt themselves really badly.
- ☐ A student on 'Young Sports Stars' hurt himself.

b
- ☐ It was good to be home again.
- ☑ It helped that I didn't have to mix with the bullies.
- ☐ It helped to be with the bullies for months and months.

c
- ☐ Talking won't help you.
- ☑ It helps to tell other people about your problems.
- ☐ Never talk too much about other people.

d ✓ Everybody can be bullied.

☐ Only some students are bullied.

☐ Bullying can't happen to anyone.

39 **a** In social studies they learned about **political conflicts**.

b In geography he learned about **mountains, rivers, countries, cities**, …

c In history he learned about **wars, kings and queens, international conflicts**, …

d In biology he learned about **plants, animals, people's health**, …

e In mathematics he learned about **numbers, shapes, geometric figures**, …

40 **a** newspaper

b magazine

c mobile

d picture book

41

get …	make …	keep …
… divorced	… a mess	… a promise
… **married**	… **the bed**	… **a secret**
… **dressed**	… **a mistake**	… **someone waiting**
… **angry**	… **tea or coffee**	… **quiet**
… **a job**		

42 **a** Last year even my friends **bullied** me at school.

b I **was** very shocked.

c So I **told** my mother and my teacher.

d Talking **made** things better.

e I **felt** terrible being bullied.

43 **a** Pete **was** in 'Young Sports Stars' when they **bullied** him at school.

b It **shocked** Pete that some of the bullies **were** his friends.

c The bullying **went on** for months and it **got** worse.

d He **didn't want** to leave his class.

e The Head **put** him in a room next to hers.

f It **helped** Pete being on his own.

g The bullies **forgot** Pete after the summer holidays.

44   On Monday Pete e-mailed the studio.
On Tuesday he **met Sam at the studio**.
On Wednesday he **went to a theatre performance at the youth club**.
On Thursday he **watched the match Arsenal London vs. Leeds United on TV**.
On Friday he **played tennis with Mike**.
On Saturday he **visited his Grandma**.
On Sunday he **phoned Olivia**, but he **didn't plan his next holiday in Paris** or **learn French**.

45   'Yesterday I had a lot to do: First I **cooked / prepared** a meal for her. Then I **did** the shopping. I **bought** milk, tea and bread. Grandma **slept** till 3 o'clock. I **watered** the flowers. Afterwards I **tried** to repair Grandma's TV set but I **couldn't** do it. I hope Grandma will be OK soon.'

46   a   I don't like talk shows on TV.
   b   I don't mind somebody teasing me.
   c   I can't stand / I hate someone bullying a classmate.
   d   I hope you'll solve the conflicts soon.
   e   Best wishes to you.

47

Dear Alice,

Thank you for your long e-mail and the invitation to London.
I'll visit you as soon as possible and I'll bring my friend … with me. We have already started to save money for the flight.
I'm sorry that your classmates bullied you because of the quiz show on TV.
I think it was sensible (wise), that you talked to your parents, the teachers and the headmaster at once.
In my class, a classmate named Patrick was bullied, too, because he trains in a very famous football club. Even his best friends were very jealous. They teased him, it got worse and worse, and nobody helped him.
There were mediators at my old school. Every student could talk to them about his/her problems. The mediators solved the conflict between the football star and his classmates with words, so nobody got hurt. Patrick hasn't been bullied any more afterwards.

I'm sorry (that) I couldn't help you. I hope nobody will bully you in the future any more.

Please write back soon! Give my regards to your parents,

Yours …

Topic 5: Sasha

48 Tick (✓) the right answer.

a Sasha and Tina met . . .

- [ ] when Sasha made her first record.
- [✓] a long time ago.
- [ ] after Sasha had made lots of records.
- [ ] a few weeks ago.

b Sasha and Tina both . . .

- [ ] like the same music.
- [ ] have normal lives.
- [ ] make records.
- [✓] like the same make-up.

c Sasha and Tina talk about . . .

- [ ] boys.
- [ ] what happens when Sasha is travelling.
- [ ] music.
- [✓] what happens at school.

d Sasha . . .

- [✓] doesn't think singing is all-important.
- [ ] thinks that singing is the most important thing in the world.
- [ ] wants to continue singing all her life.
- [ ] wants to stop singing.

e Tina says that . . .

- [ ] Sasha thinks about boys all the time.
- [ ] none of the boys want to speak to Sasha.
- [✓] more boys want to talk to Sasha than to her.
- [ ] Sasha isn't worried about her hair.

f Tina says that Sasha …

- ☐ doesn't have to go to school.
- ☐ has two teachers at school.
- ☐ is jealous of other girls at school.
- ☑ is good at her schoolwork.

g Tina and Sasha …

- ☐ have been to New York together.
- ☑ have been on holiday together.
- ☐ have spent all of Sasha's money.
- ☐ only have two other friends.

49

A	B	C	D
3	4	2	1

50

Sasha	Tina	Sasha and Tina	
		☑	… never argue.
☑			… travels a lot.
	☑		… has a brother.
		☑	… like the same jewellery.
☑			… earns a lot of money.
		☑	… plan a trip to the Caribbean.

51 **a**
- ☐ They're best friends because of Sasha's fame and money.
- ☑ Success hasn't changed Sasha.
- ☐ Tina is jealous.

b
- ☐ I've never done it all.
- ☑ It hasn't become normal for me to be a star.
- ☐ It helped that I've grown used to be a star.

c
- ☐ She's always been worried about her hair.
- ☑ She's always been optimistic.
- ☐ She's always been self-conscious.

52

autumn	**fall**
lift	elevator
film	**movie**
holidays	vacation
luggage	**baggage**
lorry	**truck**
taxi	cab
underground	**subway**
motorway	highway
petrol station	**gas station**

53 singer, musician, drummer, pop group, guitar-player, guitar, drum sticks, drums, radio station, loudspeakers, listen to, pop concert, musical instruments, . . .

54 A florist works in a flower shop.
A car mechanic repairs cars.
A baker makes bread and cakes.
A website designer makes websites for the internet.
An astronaut flies a rocket.
An office clerk types letters, organises meetings.
A vet looks after sick animals.
A nurse helps sick people.
A bricklayer builds houses.
A window dresser decorates shop windows.

55 **a** Have you ever had grapefruit juice before? – Yes, **I've often drunk / had it**.
b Have **you ever eaten bacon, eggs and grilled tomatoes** for breakfast? – No, I haven't.
c **Have you ever drunk English tea?** – No, at home we drink Chinese tea.
d **Have you ever tried scones with clotted cream?** – No. **I've never tried** scones with clotted cream before. But I would like to try them.

56 **a** A thief has broken the shop window.
      b A boy has lost his purse.
      c A dog has bitten the postman.
      d Somebody has dropped a pair of trainers on the ground.
      e A young man has had an accident.

57 **a** Tina, have you ever been to Australia?
      b I've never visited the USA.
      c Has Sasha ever tried mountain biking?
      d I've never been to a school disco.
      e My friend hasn't called for two weeks.

58 Cartoon

In the cartoon you see a boy and a girl. They are walking on the pavement in opposite directions. Both are looking at their smartphones, writing messages. It seems the boy and the girl know each other because in the speech bubbles you can read that they are writing "How's it going, Rachel?" and "Good, Kyle." However, instead of just talking face to face they prefer to send text messages. Maybe the boy and the girl haven't even noticed that they passed each other.
The cartoonist wants to show (in an exaggerated way) that the smartphone has changed the way people communicate. There is a lot of communication via text messages or social media nowadays, although talking on the phone or meeting in person would be much nicer.

Topic 6: Sadiq's journey

59   Tick (✓) the right answer.

a   Sadiq's family ...

☐ went to England with him.

✓ stayed in Afghanistan.

☐ couldn't give him any money.

☐ spent the rest of their lives in a camp.

b   Sadiq travelled through Iran ...

☐ on foot.

☐ by truck.

☐ by car.

✓ by bus.

c   Sadiq got into Turkey ...

☐ without too much trouble.

✓ although it wasn't safe.

☐ quickly.

☐ on his own.

d   Sadiq worked in a factory in Istanbul so that he could ...

☐ buy clothes.

☐ send money to his family.

☐ pay for a long ride on a truck.

✓ get on a boat and leave Turkey.

e   On board there ...

✓ were lots of people.

☐ were some dead people.

☐ were Greek soldiers.

☐ was plenty to eat and drink.

f Sadiq travelled from Greece to London by …

☐ bus, train and plane.

☑ boat, train and truck.

☐ boat, bicycle and bus.

☐ car, plane and truck.

g In Rome Sadiq hid in a lorry when …

☐ the driver washed it.

☐ the police searched it.

☑ no-one noticed.

☐ it was dark.

60

A	B	C	D
3	1	4	2

61 **a** He crossed Pakistan and Iran by bus.
b In Istanbul he worked in a **clothing factory**.
c On a large fishing boat he left for **Italy**.
d On a military boat he travelled to a **Greek island**.
e In Italy he took a **train** to **Rome**.
f On his way to **Britain** he hid inside a **truck**.
g In London he contacted his **family**.

62 **a** ☑ 'We have to decide to stay here for the rest of our lives or to sell our land.'

☐ 'We sell the land and spend the rest of our lives in this camp.'

☐ 'If we sell the land we will still have to stay in the camp.'

b ☐ They had problems on their way through Iran.

☐ Crossing Iran was dangerous.

☑ It wasn't difficult for him to travel through Iran.

c ☑ The refugees were safe on the Greek military boat.

☐ The people on the large fishing boat were hungry.

☐ He cried when he was rescued by Greek soldiers.

d ☑ He had no choice. He had to hide in the truck or the police would have caught him.

☐ The police caught him when he got in a truck in Italy.

☐ He hid inside a truck but somebody saw him.

e ☐ He works every night.

☑ He tries to earn money to help his family far away.

☐ He likes his job in an all-night shop in south London.

63 people – rescued – refugees – food – dangerous

64 bus, coach, car, bike, motorbike, scooter, van, caravan, trailer, truck, tanker, plane, helicopter, train, underground train, ferry, fishing boat, military boat, …

65

basket
vase
safe
purse
bin
box
school bag
suitcase
envelope

flowers
coins
exercise books
shopping
washing powder
jewellery, secret documents
clothes
letter
waste paper

66 **a** **As soon as** the Taliban put his father in prison his family escaped to a refugee camp in Pakistan.

b **After that** Sadiq started his dangerous journey.

c He worked in Istanbul **in order to** earn some money for the boat trip to Italy.

d **As soon as** he had enough money he left on a large fishing boat for Italy.

e In Rome he got inside a truck to Britain **while** no-one was looking.

f Finally, he arrived in London safely **although** it was a very long and dangerous journey.

67 **a** I work hard in order to pass my final exams.

b I'll meet my friends when I've got time.

c I often go to the cinema although I get little pocket money.

d I go downhill skiing as soon as it snows in the mountains.

e First I buy a present then I'll go to the birthday party.

68
  a   Hello, this is … speaking.
  b   I'm sorry for all people who live in refugee camps.
  c   I think all people on earth should be free and equal.
  d   I hope I'll see my family soon.
  e   Can you tell me which job I should choose?
  f   I'm not afraid of the interview.
  g   I'm not worried about my future.

69

> Thomas Mayr
> Birkenweg 7
> 80355 München
> Germany
>
> Mrs Vera Brown
> Personnel Manager Adventure Lake District
> 157 Jeffrey Hill Close
> Preston
> PRR 67Z
> Great Britain
>
> September 15th, 20…
>
> Dear Mrs Brown,
>
> I am … years old and attend the … Mittelschule in … I'll finish school in July … and I'll start an apprenticeship as a gardener.
>
> Our English teacher at school told us about the summer camp in the Lake District. I am writing to apply for a 3-week-job in August … I would like to work as a gardener. I'm very interested in the job. In Germany, I worked in a car factory for 2 weeks last April, so I really know how to work hard.
>
> I speak German and English. I enclose my curriculum vitae/cv. I hope you will consider my application and I look forward to hearing from you soon.
>
> Yours sincerely,
>
> *Thomas Mayr*
> Thomas Mayr

Topic 7: Alicia's World Tour Diary

70 Tick (✓) the right answer.

a On arrival Alicia feels …

- [✓] a bit tired.
- [ ] bored.
- [ ] calm.
- [ ] hot.

b Frank has just given Alicia …

- [ ] a message.
- [ ] a present.
- [✓] a massage.
- [ ] a tour guide.

c Alicia isn't going shopping today because …

- [ ] of the weather.
- [ ] she couldn't wait.
- [ ] of her lunch.
- [✓] of the concert.

d At the sound-check Alicia …

- [ ] does an interview.
- [✓] makes sure everything is OK.
- [ ] has some sleep.
- [ ] has something to eat.

e After her tuna salad Alicia …

- [ ] sees lots of friends.
- [ ] has a massage.
- [✓] gets ready for her show.
- [ ] still feels hungry.

f Alicia prepares for her concert by …

- [ ] drinking orange juice.
- [ ] changing her songs.
- [ ] washing herself.
- [✓] singing some songs.

g Before the show starts Alicia …

- [✓] stands in a circle with her dancers.
- [ ] sings to her security guy.
- [ ] holds hands with Rob.
- [ ] goes for a long walk.

71

A	B	C	D
3	1	4	2

72 **a** Alicia is ~~Australian~~ **American**.
  b Alicia arrived in Great Britain ~~two days ago~~ **yesterday**.
  c She thinks the ~~meals~~ **shops** in London are really hot.
  d The sound-check takes place ~~after~~ **before** the concert.
  e She ~~dislikes~~ **loves / likes / enjoys** having a massage.
  f With Rob, her ~~fitness trainer~~ **security guy**, she walks to the side of the stage.
  g Alicia is nervous, it's her ~~second~~ **first** world tour.
  h She always drinks so much ~~cola~~ **water**.
  i She starts warming up by singing a few songs to ~~cool down~~ **warm up** her voice.

73

7	She walked to the stage with Rob, her security guy. (l. 32)
3	She had some sleep. (l. 20)
4	She did an interview for radio. (l. 20 f.)
6	She warmed her voice up by singing some of her songs. (l. 27)
8	Alicia and her dancers held hands to get themselves ready. (l. 32 f.)
2	She went to the sound-check. (l. 15)
1	She had a massage. (l. 6 f.)
5	She ate a small tuna salad. (l. 23)

74

Fans
- **watch** TV interviews and video clips.
- **visit** Alicia's homepage.
- **read** magazines and newspaper articles about Alicia.
- **love** Alicia's music best.
- **listen to** her radio interviews.
- **send** e-mails to her.
- **wear** a T-shirt with her photo every day.
- **go to** her concerts.
- **find out** everything about Alicia.

75

voice	9	the sounds that you make when you speak
favourite	7	what you like best
excited	5	very happy because something good is going to happen
stage	3	where singers or actors perform
make sure	2	to do what is necessary for something to happen
circle	1	a round geometric figure
diary	4	a book where you write what happens every day

76

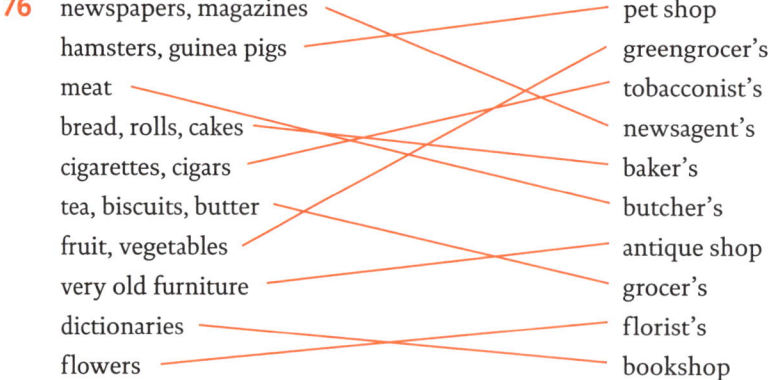

newspapers, magazines — newsagent's
hamsters, guinea pigs — pet shop
meat — butcher's
bread, rolls, cakes — baker's
cigarettes, cigars — tobacconist's
tea, biscuits, butter — grocer's
fruit, vegetables — greengrocer's
very old furniture — antique shop
dictionaries — bookshop
flowers — florist's

77

biscuit	**cookie**
bill	check
queue	**line**
post	mail
toilet	restroom
one-way ticket	**single ticket**
rucksack	backpack
shop	store
pullover	sweater
rubber	**eraser**

78 **a** Diana is cooking for her friends **eagerly**.
b Tony is watching the football match **lazily**.
c Ian is looking forward to the musical **excitedly**.
d Mary is celebrating her birthday **happily**.

79

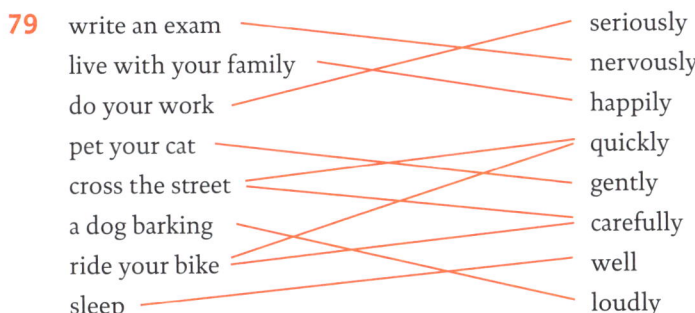

80 It was a lovely day in September. The sun was shining **brightly**, a light breeze was blowing **gently** and the birds were singing **beautifully**, but Mariah didn't notice. She was worried because her work was going **badly** and her boss was terrible. As she was walking **slowly** down the road she met her friend Brian. He was on his way to his pub. They talked **seriously** about her problems. In the end Brian asked her to work at his pub. Mariah accepted his offer **happily**. What a lovely day for her.

81 **a** May / Can / Could I speak / talk to . . .
    b Can / Could you put me through to . . .
    c I'll call again later.
    d Can / Could / Would you take a message, please?
       Will you give him / her a message, please?
    e Could you phone / call me back?
    f Hold on, I'll get her for you.
       Hold on, I'll put you through to my mother.
    g Sorry, Mom is not at home
       She isn't in at the moment.
    h Could / Can / Would you call again later?
    i Thanks / Thank you for calling / phoning.
    j Could you please spell your internet address?
    k Sorry, I didn't get that. Could you please repeat it?

82 Sarah's story

Sarah is a big fan of Alicia – she really loves her favourite singer's music. She is writing in her diary: 'I love Alicia.'

Two weeks ago she saw a big poster at the railway station: *Alicia's World Tour – concert at Wembley on July 8th.* Sarah was very happy! The next day she took all her pocket money, went to the ticket counter and bought a ticket for the concert. At a department store she bought/found/got a wonderful/nice/lovely Alicia-T-shirt.

A week later she wrote in her diary: 'Today is the big day. I'm very excited. Today I'm going to see HER with my own eyes.' In the afternoon she put on her make-up very carefully in front of the mirror and put on her Alicia-T-shirt. She then took the underground to Wembley.

A little later she arrived at the underground station in Wembley – but there were only a few people around. Sarah was surprised and a bit worried. 'Maybe the concert is cancelled? Maybe there's something wrong with Alicia??? Oh, no, I hope not!!' she thought.

When she arrived at the ticket counter at Wembley Stadium a friendly lady explained: 'Today is July 7th, you're too early for the Alicia concert – it is tomorrow.'

'Thank God – everything is okay. It's only my fault. I didn't check my calendar.' Sarah thought. 'I'll be here tomorrow, then.' Sarah told the lady at the counter and they both smiled.

Topic 8: Valentine Day's Visit

83 Tick (✓) the right answer.

a Teresa was sad because …

☐ she was alone.

☐ she hadn't got a Valentine card.

☐ it was Valentine's Day.

☑ her mother had died.

b Teresa had to stay …

☑ with her uncle now.

☐ in Baltimore.

☐ in her mother's room.

☐ with her brother in Washington.

c Teresa wanted …

☐ the war in Vietnam to end.

☐ her brother to leave the army.

☑ her brother to help her.

☐ her uncle to help her move.

d Jimmy and Teresa packed …

☑ Teresa's things.

☐ their mother's things.

☐ the mover's things.

☐ their uncle's things.

e While they were waiting for the truck the brother and sister …

☑ didn't talk to each other.

☐ talked a lot.

☐ talked about the war in Vietnam.

☐ talked about their mother.

f Teresa's telegram said that Jimmy …

☐ had to go back to Vietnam.

☐ wasn't going to Washington with her.

☑ died on Valentine's day.

☐ was with her in Washington.

		true	false	not in the text
84	**a** Teresa was a 20-year-old girl living in Baltimore.	☐	☑	☐
	b Teresa was crying because she didn't get a Valentine card.	☐	☑	☐
	c Her mother was buried in Baltimore.	☐	☐	☑
	d Teresa had to move out of the apartment.	☑	☐	☐
	e She had to live alone in Washington now.	☐	☑	☐
	f Teresa's brother was serving with the army in Vietnam.	☑	☐	☐
	g Her brother called a mover who could take her and her things to Washington.	☐	☑	☐
	h Her brother helped put everything in the mover's truck.	☑	☐	☐
	i As the truck left Teresa's brother decided to go to Washington with her.	☐	☑	☐
	j Teresa's brother had died on his way to Baltimore on February 14th.	☐	☑	☐
	k Jimmy was buried in Baltimore like his mother.	☐	☐	☑

85 Individual answers. Examples:

I think ghost stories are nonsense. There are no ghosts around. People sometimes have the impression of magic happening, but it is only in their imagination.

or:

I believe in ghost stories because I have often seen strange things happening. Nobody could explain why they happened. So there must be something we can't explain like ghosts or black magic.

86
a	old	**new**
b	**sad /unhappy**	happy
c	**interesting /exciting**	boring
d	**liked /loved**	hated
e	lazy	**busy /active**
f	**heavy**	light
g	**fast**	slowly
h	alive	**dead**

87

88
  a There's a cat in the tree over there. Can you **see** it?
  b I'm afraid not. I cannot **see** very well. I need glasses.
  c Oh, please be careful! **Watch** out for cars when you cross the street.
  d Philip, please switch on the light. I can't **see** what I'm reading any longer.
  e Haven't you got eyes in your head, little boy? Why don't you **look** where you're going?
  f On the phone: Peter, can you come and **see** me next Saturday?
  g We could have dinner and **watch** TV afterwards.
  h Do you like to **watch** sports on TV?

89 Tina's uncle, who is thirty-five years older than she is, **loves** Elvis Presley's music. He **buys** a lot of singles and CDs. He **says**: "I think Elvis Presley's music **is** great." But Tina usually **doesn't like** Rock'n'Roll. She **prefers** modern pop music. She often **goes** to concerts of her favourite band.

90 **a** **How old are you?** I'm eighteen.

     b **Where do you live?** In Washington.

     c **Do you live alone?** No, I live with my uncle.

     d **What are your hobbies?** I listen to pop music, read books and watch TV.

     e **Do you have a brother?** Yes, his name is Jimmy.

91 A is reading a newspaper.

     B is drinking a cup of coffee.

     C is waiting for the bus.

     D is eating a sandwich.

     E is looking at a map.

     F is using a mobile phone.

     G is taking a photo.

92 **a** Teresa is **sitting** alone in her apartment.

     b She is **waiting** for a Valentine card.

     c Teresa **is crying** because her mother died two weeks ago.

     d Teresa **is wiping** her tears from her eyes.

     e She **is packing** her mother's clothes and possessions.

93 **a** How are you?

     b Are you worried about your job?

     c What do you think of part-time jobs?

     d I think you should talk to your parents.

     e Have you got any plans?

     f How important is a well-paid job for you?

     g I promise to help you find a job.

94 Black Magic?

On February 14th, Valentine's Day, Sandra was very happy. She got a nice Valentine card from her new boyfriend Kevin. In the evening she talked to Kevin on the telephone and invited him for an evening meal on Friday. He was very pleased.

On Friday, Sandra was very excited. She laid the table and prepared a delicious meal – grilled fish with potatoes and mixed salad – for her candle-light-dinner. Then the doorbell rang. It was Kevin. He had a bunch of lovely flowers in his hands.

They entered the dining-room to have their meal. When Sandra looked at the table she couldn't believe her eyes – there was only one plate with grilled fish, the second plate was empty!

Sandra was worried and puzzled. She knew she had put two plates of fish on the table. What had happened? Was it black magic?

Kevin put his arms around her and said: 'Calm down, Sandra. There are no ghosts.' He went to the table and lifted the tablecloth. Blacky, her cat, was under the table, and there were some bits of fish on the floor. Blacky was the black 'ghost' who stole the fish!

Sandra and Kevin shared the rest of their meal and enjoyed the evening after all.

Topic 9: Body Piercing

95   Tick (✓) the right answer.

a   Sarah wants ...

- [✓] a hole in her tongue.
- [ ] a hole in her nose.
- [ ] an argument with her mother.
- [ ] a silver ring.

b   Tracy says that Sarah can ...

- [ ] never have a piercing.
- [ ] have a piercing when she's 38.
- [ ] have a piercing now.
- [✓] have a piercing in a few years' time

c   Sarah says that she ...

- [ ] will have the piercing at school.
- [✓] won't do what her mother tells her.
- [ ] won't win the argument.
- [ ] knows that her mother will win the argument.

d   In Britain you can do body piercing ...

- [ ] when you're over 18.
- [ ] when you're with your parents.
- [✓] whatever age you are.
- [ ] only when you're in a shop.

e   The shop owner, Ali, says that ...

- [ ] all the body piercing shops are the same.
- [ ] he helps teenagers to pierce themselves.
- [✓] body piercing can be very dangerous.
- [ ] it's better for parents to do the body piercing.

f 'Temptoos' can last for …

- [✓] no more than seven years.
- [ ] three hours.
- [ ] 18 years.
- [ ] ever.

g Roger Cooey says that the law on body piercing …

- [✓] should be up to date.
- [ ] is fine as it is.
- [ ] causes no problems.
- [ ] makes parents pierce themselves.

		true	false	not in the text
96	**a** Body piercing is the latest fashion for teenagers.	✓		
	b It can be dangerous to pierce your body yourself.	✓		
	c There are many shops specialised in piercing all over the UK.			✓
	d There is no law about body piercing in the UK.	✓		
	e You can do body piercing to adults only.		✓	
	f To get a real 'tattoo' you'll have to wait till you're 18.	✓		
	g A 'smile gem' is a diamond stuck on the ears.		✓	

97

98

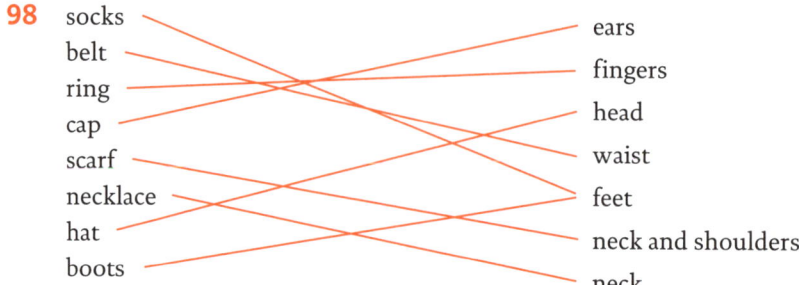

socks	ears
belt	fingers
ring	head
cap	waist
scarf	feet
necklace	neck and shoulders
hat	neck
boots	

99 **a** Have you already made an appointment for the body piercing next Friday?
b No, I haven't because I didn't have enough time.

100

A	B	C	D	E	F
2	4	6	5	3	1

101 **a** If Sarah has time on Saturday, **she'll go** shopping.
b If Sarah has enough money for trendy shoes, **she'll buy** some.
c If it starts to rain, **she won't go** to the beach.
d If she feels hungry, **she'll get / she'll eat** a sandwich.
e If her mother can't find her credit card, **she'll pay** cash.
f If Sarah repairs her bike herself, **she'll save** money.
g If she sells old toys at a flea market, **she'll get** some money.
h If Sarah doesn't hurry, **she'll miss** the bus.

102 **a** If my parents allow it, I'll have a piercing.
b My friend Caro wasn't allowed to buy smile gems.
c I think permanent tattoos aren't ideal for young people.

103

Dear Sarah,

Thank you for your e-mail.
I can understand your problem very well. I have another friend, who would like to get her tongue pierced. Her parents won't let her until she's 18.
I think you should wait until your 18th birthday. I wouldn't start a quarrel with my parents over a piercing.
Why don't you go to a shop which specialises in body piercing to have your ears pierced? I would never pierce my ears myself. I read in a teenage magazine that it is very dangerous and can cause blood poisoning if you pierce yourself.
Well, when I'm 18, I'd like to go on holiday without my parents. I'd like to have my own little flat and I'd like to have a dog.
I'm sorry I couldn't help you. I also have to ask my parents if I want to go out in the evening, for example. I often discuss problems with them and I can talk to my mother about almost everything.
I hope you'll get on well with your parents.

Write back soon and give my regards to your parents,

yours …

Checkpoint

Wenn du mit einer Aufgabe Schwierigkeiten hattest, wiederhole die Grammatik des Topics. Das Symbol → verweist auf die entsprechende Stelle im Buch.

104 a Alaska is **colder than** Florida.
  b Antarctica is **the coldest** place in the world.
  c Death Valley is **the hottest** place in the USA.
  d Mont Blanc is **the highest** mountain in Europe.
  e Mount Everest is **higher than** Mont Blanc.
  f The Nile is **the longest** river in the world.
  g The river Rhine is **longer than** the river Thames.
  h Washington is **smaller than** New York.
  i London is **bigger than** Edinburgh.
  j The Mona Lisa is **the most famous** painting in the world.
→ „Vergleich und Steigerung von Adjektiven", S. 6 f.

105 a My father is **as old as** my mother.
  b What do you think? Is stealing **worse than** telling lies?
  c This year my English teacher is very pleased, because my English is **not as bad as** last year.
  d I find maths **not as difficult as** physics.
  e My new mountain bike was **more expensive than** yours.
  f I think the Queen is one of **the richest** persons in the world.
  g For me Euro Disney is **the greatest** tourist attraction in Paris.
  h That was **the worst** book I've ever read.
  i *Titanic* is **the best** Hollywood film I've ever seen.
  j It's **the most difficult** exam I've ever taken.
→ „Vergleich und Steigerung von Adjektiven", S. 6 f.

106 a If Michael's parents let him, he **will have** 50 guests at the party.
  b He wonders whether his friends **will bring** him any presents.
  c Michael is good at organising things and he will **not/won't make** any mistakes in planning his party.
  d Mr Brown, Michael's father, **will not/won't be** at the party on Saturday.
  e He is on a business trip to London so he **will not/won't celebrate** Michael's birthday with him.
→ „Die Zukunft mit *will*", S. 17

107 **a** Will the weather be nice tomorrow?

b It will probably rain tomorrow.

c If it rains, the party will be indoors.

d She has saved enough money. She will buy a new car soon.

e If you drive drunk, you'll lose your driving licence.

f If you do sports regularly, you'll stay fit.

→ „Die Zukunft mit *will*", S. 17, und „Der Bedingungssatz", S. 92.

108 **a** **Have you left** school yet? – Yes, I have.

b **Have you ever visited** Australia? – No, I've never been there.

c But I **went** to Florida and California last summer.

d How much **did you pay** for your trip to the USA? Oh, it was terribly expensive, but my parents were very helpful.

e **Have you seen** our old friend Claire recently? Yes, I **met** her yesterday evening at her apartment.

f Imagine – She **prepared** a five-course-meal for me yesterday.

g The meal **was** delicious last night.

h I **came** home very late last Friday.

i Oh, look! I **have just got** another message from her.

j That's ten messages today. I think she **has fallen** in love with me.

→ „Die 1. Vergangenheit", S. 35, und „Die 2. Vergangenheit", S. 48.

109 At the moment she's doing her exercises at the fitness studio.

Last year she got a job with a drama company.

She hopes she'll act in a famous musical one day.

Every morning she jogs in the park.

When she was a schoolgirl she was bullied by her classmates because she always wore unfashionable clothes.

Since she was young she has wanted to be a Hollywood actress.

110 I've arrived in London safely and the weather is really nice. It's **both** warm **and** sunny. **Although** my hotel is quite cheap it's in the centre and close to an underground station. I had to take a room without a private bathroom **because** it was the only one left. You can also get Wi-Fi access at the hotel **as long as** you are a guest there. I want to write some e-mails, **but** I've forgotten my address book. Could you look for it? Please bring it with you. The sights are great **so** don't forget your new camera.

→ „Bindewörter", S. 60.

111 **a** It looks **as if** it will rain soon.
b We had to put on the heating **because** it was a very cold day.
c I have saved enough money **so** I can now afford to buy a digital camera.
d I've worked for this company **ever since** I left university.
e You can have a garden party **as long as** the neighbours don't complain about the noise.
f You can go skating **as soon as** you finish your homework.
g I worked very hard **in order to** pass my exams.
h He smiled **but** he didn't say a word.

→ „Bindewörter", S. 60.

112 **a** I have **my** own mountain bike now.
b I paid for it **myself**.
c Your mountain bike was cheaper than **mine**.
d John had an accident, he broke **his** arm.
e Have you repaired John's bike? – No, he can do it **himself**.
f Will you clean my bike? – No, I won't. Clean it **yourself**.
g If you don't clean **my** bike, I'll clean it **myself**.
h In the evening the other cyclists often forget to take **their** lights with **them**.
i John and I often go to mountain bike races and today Mary came with **us**. We all enjoy **ourselves** very much.
j John's brother is a great mountain biker. Look at **him**. **He** really cycles fast. **His** will be the best time.

→ „Fürwörter", S. 26 f.

113 a If you like travelling, you'll enjoy this book.

     b If you look in the telephone directory, you'll find my number.

     c If I don't know the meaning of a word, I'll use a dictionary.

     d If you feed the animals, the zoo attendant will be very angry.

     e If Tom needs advice, he'll talk to a teacher.

     f I won't go swimming if it's too cold.

     g If you book a flight last-minute, you'll get it cheaper.

     h If you can't speak English, you won't get the job.

     i If I promise to drive carefully, will you let me borrow your motorbike?

→ „Der Bedingungssatz", S. 92.

114 a Susan plays tennis **badly**.

     b She dances **wonderfully**.

     c He works **slowly**.

     d But he drives **carefully**.

     e They don't learn **quickly**.

     f They play the piano **well**.

→ „Adverbien", S. 71.

Bildnachweis

Wir danken allen Rechtinhabern für die Abdruckerlaubnis. Der Verlag hat sich bemüht, die Urheber aller abgedruckten Bilder ausfindig zu machen. Wo dies nicht gelungen ist, bitten wir diese, sich ggf. an den Verlag zu wenden.

Umschlag: © oneinchpunch. Shutterstock

S. 1: © Can Stock Photo Inc./dolgachov
S. 2: © Jean-Charles Pinheira
S. 7: © c-foto. 123rf.com
S. 10: © bloomua. Shutterstock
S. 11: © Deutsches Fernerkundungsdatenzentrum, Oberpfaffenhofen www.dfd.dlr.de
S. 13: © Nalukai/Dreamstime.com
S. 17: © M. Unal Ozmen. Shutterstock
S. 20: © kaarsten. Shutterstock
S. 26: © Kopfhörer © Kazlouski Siarhei. Shutterstock, Smartphones © scanrail. 123rf.com
S. 27: © 63555. Shutterstock
S. 28: © Absolut_photos/Dreamstime.com
S. 29: © Chode/Dreamstime.com
S. 30: © Deutsches Jugendrotkreuz
S. 40: © Joegough/Dreamstime.com
S. 42: © Jose Manuel Gelpi Diaz/Dreamstime.com
S. 46: © Vladimir Mucibabic/Dreamstime.com
S. 47: © Floristin © kurhan. Shutterstock, Maurer © bogdanhoda. Shutterstock, Computertastatur © 2066807. Shutterstock
S. 48: Abb. nach Josef Meier: Mehr Freude und Erfolg beim Englischlernen mit innovativen Lern- und Mentaltechniken, München, IBS Verlag, S. 219
S. 50: © Indos82/Dreamstime.com (USA und Australien)
S. 51: © Carl Durocher/Dreamstime.com
S. 52: © Dave Carpenter/Cartoonstock.com
S. 54: © Yali Shi/Dreamstime.com
S. 56: © Photoblueice/Dreamstime.com
S. 63: Stift © Claudio Bertoloni. Shutterstock
S. 64: © Adrian Fortune/Dreamstime.com
S. 65: © Jason Stitt/Dreamstime.com; © Jurie Maree/Dreamstime.com
S. 66: © Jason Stitt/Dreamstime.com
S. 77: © Dmitry Remesov-Fotolia.com
S. 88: © Blphotocorp/Dreamstime.com
S. 94: © Nikolai Sorokin/Dreamstime.com
S. 95: © biglama-Fotolia.com
S. 97: © 123rf.com
S. 98: © Can Stock Photo/sdecoret
S. 100: © 123rf.com
S. 101: Smartphone © Bloomua. Shutterstock, Herz © tackgalichstudio. 123rf.com
S. 102: © Can Stock Photo/whitewizzard
S. 105: © Dmitry Lobanov. Shutterstock
S. 107: © Young Kimpark/Dreamstime.com
S. 115: © Les Cunliffe/Dreamstime.com

STOPP DIE
PANIK

Mit der Fußsohlen-Methode

Prüfungen können Angst- und Fluchtsituationen sein. Dein Körper schüttet Adrenalin aus und dämpft das Gefühl in den Füßen. Z. B. beim Weglaufen ist es gut, wenn man die Füße nicht spürt. Eine Prüfung ist aber **keine Gefahrensituation**. Signalisiere deinem Körper, dass du nicht weglaufen musst, und bring das Gefühl in deine Füße zurück:

Setze oder stelle dich hin.
Die Füße müssen den **Boden** berühren.

Schließe jetzt deine Augen und **denke** dich in deine Füße hinein.

jeden einzelnen **Zeh**
von klein s p ü r e bis **groß**.

Erkunde den **Bogen** deines Fußes.

Fahre in Gedanken um die **Fersen**.

Spüre den **Druck** auf dem Boden.

Dein Körper **fühlt** die Füße wieder und denkt, er sei in keiner Panik-Situation, sondern in **Sicherheit**.

Bist du bereit für deinen Einstellungstest?

Hier kannst du testen, wie gut du in einem Einstellungstest zurechtkommen würdest.

1. Allgemeinwissen
Der Baustil des Kölner Doms ist dem/der ... zuzuordnen.

a) Klassizismus   b) Romantizismus
c) Gotik   d) Barock

2. Wortschatz
Welches Wort ist das?

N O R I N E T K T A Z N O

3. Grundrechnen
-11 + 23 - (-1) =

a) 10   b) 11   c) 12   d) 13

4. Zahlenreihen
Welche Zahl ergänzt die Reihe logisch?

17 14 7 21 18 9 ?

5. Buchstabenreihen
Welche Auswahlmöglichkeit ergänzt die Reihe logisch?

e d f f e g g f h ? ? ?

a) h i j   b) h g i   c) f g h   d) g h i

Alles zum Thema Einstellungstests findest du hier:

www.stark-verlag.de/einstellungstest **STARK**